rororo

rororo sprachen
Herausgegeben von Ludwig Moos

Drop Them a Line befasst sich mit Briefen, wie sie jeder im Beruf schreiben, lesen oder beantworten muss, der mit englischsprachigen Geschäftspartnern zu tun hat. Bewerbungen, Angebote, Beschwerden, Einladungen, Memos oder Kostenvoranschläge sind nur einige der vielen Schriftformen, deren Sprache und Stil das Buch einüben hilft. Sie lernen, wie Sie sich einfach, aber effektiv ausdrücken und zu jeder Situation im Geschäftsalltag die passende Wendung finden. Und damit der Stoff nicht zu trocken wird, ist er eingebettet in nicht allzu ernsthafte Geschichten, wie sie das Geschäftsleben schreibt.

Bryan Hemming ist Native Speaker und arbeitet als Sprachlehrer in Firmen.

Mitgearbeitet an dem Buch haben Dr. René Bosewitz und Robert Kleinschroth, von denen das Konzept und die meisten der bisher erschienenen Bände der Reihe *Business English* stammen.

René Bosewitz ist Native Speaker und bereitet in einer deutschen Zweigstelle der London Chamber of Commerce Firmenangehörige auf einschlägige sprachliche Prüfungen vor. Er trainiert zudem seit vielen Jahren Manager aus Banken und Industrie in Business English (mehr Informationen unter www.combenations.de). Bei rororo sprachen hat er *Better Your English* (60802) und *Perfect Your English* (61147) sowie zusammen mit Robert Kleinschroth *Joke Your Way Through English Grammar* (61408) und *Joke by Joke to Conversation* (18797) veröffentlicht.

Robert Kleinschroth unterrichtet Englisch am Gymnasium und an der Universität Heidelberg. Er hat zwanzig Jahre Praxis in der Erwachsenenbildung und leitete fünfzehn Jahre lang die Sprachabteilung eines Großunternehmens. Robert Kleinschroth hat zusammen mit Anne-Laure und Dieter Maupai *Flüssiges Französisch* (61184) verfasst und außerdem *Sprachen lernen* (60842) geschrieben.

Weitere Bände der Reihe *Business English* sind am Ende des Buches zu finden.

BRYAN HEMMING
UNTER MITARBEIT VON RENÉ BOSEWITZ
UND ROBERT KLEINSCHROTH

DROP THEM A LINE

BUSINESS ENGLISH IM SCHRIFTVERKEHR

Rowohlt Taschenbuch Verlag

Überarbeitete und erweiterte Neuausgabe Februar 2003
Veröffentlicht im Rowohlt Taschenbuch Verlag GmbH,
Reinbek bei Hamburg, Februar 1997

Umschlaggestaltung any.way, Wiebke Buckow
Illustration Britta Lembke
Layout Anne Drude
Satz OCR-A und Stone, PostScript QuarkXPress 3.31
Druck und Bindung Clausen & Bosse, Leck
Printed in Germany
ISBN 3 499 61463 4

Die Schreibweise entspricht den Regeln
der neuen Rechtschreibung.

Drop Them a Line macht Sie vertraut mit den wichtigsten Bereichen des geschäftlichen Briefverkehrs. Die Korrespondenz ist in eine Rahmenhandlung eingebunden und spiegelt die Entwicklung der Firma Onions wider. Onions ist ein Hersteller von Heizgeräten, der sich unbedingt vergrößern will. Sie verfolgen den Aufstieg der Firma und lernen englische Handelskorrespondenz vor dem Hintergrund des Geschäftsablaufs: Eine Anfrage geht ein, ein Angebot wird gemacht, ein Auftrag wird erteilt – wenn alles gut geht. Leider ist das nicht immer der Fall. Da werden Rechnungen nicht bezahlt, Lieferungen verzögern sich, Kunden beschweren sich, um nur einige der täglichen Pannen zu erwähnen, die viel Mühe kosten. Überdies drängt Onions mit Macht auf fremde Märkte. Nach anfänglichen Schwierigkeiten gelingt es sogar, die chinesische Mauer zu überwinden. Auf dem langen Weg der Firma bis zur Gründung einer Niederlassung im Fernen Osten werden Sie, neben manchem kleinen *joke*, die wichtigsten Wendungen des englischen Geschäftsbriefs auflesen und den zugrunde liegenden Geschäftsvorgang verstehen.

Es bietet sich an, die Kapitel in ihrer Reihenfolge zu lesen. Doch ist das Buch zugleich auch ein praktisches Nachschlagewerk. Wie auch immer Sie es nutzen, die klare Struktur erleichtert Ihnen das Lernen und Verstehen.

FOCUS: Zu Beginn eines jeden Kapitels wird eine typische Situation des Geschäftsalltags erläutert: der Auftrag, die Beschwerde, die Bewerbung ...

DIALOGUE: Die Mitarbeiter der Firma suchen im Gespräch nach einer Lösung des Problems. Aus diesem Gespräch entwickelt sich die Korrespondenz. Dadurch wird die Funktion des Briefes im Geschäftsablauf verständlich.

Drop Them A LINE: Der so entstandene Brief, mitunter auch ein Fax oder eine E-Mail, kann als Muster für die eigene Korrespondenz dienen. Wie Sie diese Vorlage Ihren Bedürfnissen anpassen können, erfahren Sie im folgenden Teil des Kapitels.

Put It ANOTHER WAY: Zu jedem Briefmuster erhalten Sie einen Vorrat alternativer Redewendungen mit ihren deutschen Bedeutungen.

VOCABULARY: Eine englisch-deutsche Wortschatzliste sorgt dafür, dass Sie alles verstehen. Es ist ganz einfach.

BRAIN WORK: Nicht ganz so einfach, aber lernintensiv! Sie sollen den Wortschatz und die typischen Wendungen des Geschäftsbriefs anwenden. Zu den Übungen finden Sie einen Schlüssel im Anhang, aber widerstehen Sie bitte der Versuchung zu schummeln.

LETTER BOX: Wenn es nicht ohne Grammatik geht, finden Sie hier die Regel und eine Übung. Daneben aber auch Hinweise zu so wichtigen Dingen wie den Möglichkeiten der Anrede oder des Briefschlusses.

LETTER FUNCTIONS: Im Anhang finden Sie ein systematisches Verzeichnis mit den wichtigsten Wendungen des englischen Geschäftsbriefs – den Baukasten für Ihre Korrespondenz.

Viel Spaß beim Korrespondieren.

PROBLEMS OF STYLE

PROBLEMS OF STYLE

Chapter 1

Contents

Joke Time

A boss was saying goodbye to her secretary after years of working together. "I'll be sorry to lose[1] you," she said. "You've been exactly[2] like my daughter[3]." "Really?" said the secretary a little surprised[4]. "Yes, you've been rude, lazy and bad-mannered[5] for all the years I've known you."

Ian Burns, the personnel manager[6] at Corbetts, said one morning to a trainee[7]: "Jones, I don't know how we will get along without you[8] but starting on the first of next month we are going to have a really good try."

1 verlieren 2 genau 3 Tochter 4 erstaunt 5 unhöflich, faul und ungezogen
6 Personalleiter 7 Auszubildender 8 ohne Sie zurechtkommen

FOCUS: Style in the business letter

When speaking English you can be informal but when writing business letters you must remember to be polite, formal but not pompous or old-fashioned. Above all keep the letter simple.

DIALOGUES: Terry gets a lesson

Corbetts is a wholesale company in England. They distribute food from the producer to small retailers, usually corner shops.
In the personnel department Mrs Brookes (**B**), the head of sales, is talking to Ian Burns (**I**), the personnel manager, about a new trainee, Terry Jones.

B: Well, I can't believe the letter that Jones wanted to send to one of our suppliers. Luckily I saw it first and stopped him sending it.

I: Why what's wrong now? I've had nothing but complaints about young Terry.

B: Here's the letter. See for yourself.

I: Let me just read that, let's see. (*Ian reads the letter*)
"Dear Bob", good start, okay,
"Thanks a lot for the offer of chocolate biscuits type 'Nutty Crunch' – especially as I like them myself. Your conditions are 20 quid for a box of fifty packets if we buy more than ten boxes. That's good because we need 12 boxes. Can you let us have them by next Wednesday? We really need them.
And another thing, the tins of baked beans you sent us last month ... they were no good. The customers complained, something about too much tomato sauce and not enough beans. Sorry, but if you can't send us better quality goods we must find somebody else to get us the beans.
Yours faithfully
Terry Jones"

Good Grief! I think I'd better have a few words with him straight away.

B: Well be careful about the words you use. Remember his dad is on the board of directors and his family is in all kinds of business around here.

Let's see what Ian Burns says to Terry (**T**).

I: Now about this letter to a supplier. Have you never written a letter before?
T: Actually yes. My girlfriend lives in Scotland and we can't afford to see each other every weekend so I write lots of letters.
I: Well, I can believe that but I'm talking about business letters. Formal commercial correspondence.
T: What was wrong with it? The spelling, the grammar?
I: No, it was the way the letter was written.
T: You mean I shouldn't have written it on the typewriter?
I: I mean the style. It was too informal, you were too friendly and too direct.
T: Well, Mr Miller in sales says you should be friendly when talking to clients.
I: That's on the phone when you already know the client. Right, let me try to help. Look here, I'll write some parts of your letter down on the left and I'll write what you should put on the right.

Put it ANOTHER WAY: Formal and informal

Here is what Ian Burns wrote.

Informal letter style	Formal letter style	German
thanks a lot for	thank you very much for	vielen Dank für
if we buy more than	if we purchase in excess of	wenn wir mehr als ... kaufen
can you let us have them?	would it be possible to receive the goods?	wäre es möglich, dass wir die Waren erhalten?
and another thing	in addition to this / furthermore	darüber hinaus
were no good	were of inferior quality	waren von minderer Qualität

sorry, but if you	we regret to say that if it	wir würden es bedauern, wenn
can't send us	is impossible to supply us with	aber sollte es Ihnen nicht möglich sein, uns ... zu liefern
we must find	we will be forced to find	wir werden gezwungen sein, zu finden
somebody else	an alternative supplier	ein anderer Lieferant
to get us beans	provide us with these goods	uns mit diesen Waren zu beliefern

d: Back to Terry Jones and Ian Burns

I: There you are, Terry. And by the way what is the supplier's second name?
T: It's Jones.
I: Well, don't you think you should call him Mr Jones since he is a supplier.
T: Maybe, but I think I should call him Bob since he is my uncle!

V VOCABULARY: To help you understand

biscuit	*Keks*
board of directors	*Vorstand*
complaint	*Beschwerde*
condition	*Bedingung*
corner shop	*Laden an der Ecke*
dad	*Papa*
department	*Abteilung*
distribute	*verteilen*

especially	*besonders*
food	*Lebensmittel*
good grief!	*mein Gott!*
head of sales	*Leiter der Verkaufsabteilung*
I'd better	*ich sollte/es wäre besser*
luckily	*zum Glück*
old-fashioned	*altmodisch*
polite	*höflich*
pompous	*schwülstig*
quid (slang for pound)	*Eier (umgangssprachlich für Geld)*
retailer	*Einzelhändler*
spelling	*Rechtschreibung*
supplier	*Lieferant*
tin of baked beans	*Dose mit gebackenen Bohnen*
trainee	*Auszubildende/r*
wholesale	*Großhandel*

BRAIN WORK One: Let's practise style

Here is another letter from Terry. Now it is your turn to put the style right. Below you can see some phrases. Try and put them into the letter to make it more formal.

to provide us with the goods	thank you very much for
were of inferior quality	if we purchase in excess of
an alternative supplier	in addition to this
we will be forced to find	

Dear Miss Weakley

Thanks a lot for **(1)** the offer of frozen vegetables. The price is £7.50 for a five kilo bag *if we buy more than* **(2)** 50 bags. *And another thing* **(3)** we must say is that the first class English beef burgers *were no good* **(4)**. We regret to say that if it is impossible to supply us with better quality products *we must find* **(5)** *somebody* **(6)** *to get us the beef burgers* **(7)**.

Yours faithfully

LETTER BOX: Starting and ending a letter

You can start a letter with Dear Sir, Dear Sirs, Dear Madam, Dear Mrs Jackson, Dear Snuggy Pops, Dear Sue, My Dearest Darling, To the World's Greatest Lover etc. Please do not forget it is important to follow the rule below. Also note that we do not normally address the bank manager 'Snuggy Pops'. Of course this depends on your bank manager and you. Remember!

Dear Sir	starts a letter to a man whose name you do not know.
Dear Madam	starts a letter to a woman whose name you do not know
Dear Sirs	starts a letter to a company.
Dear Sir or Madam	starts a letter where you do not know the name or sex.
And the letter ends with	*Yours faithfully.*

When you know the name of the person you are writing to start with:

Dear Mr Beavis
Dear Dr Johnson
Dear Mrs Whitehouse

And the letter ends with *Yours sincerely.*

Do not start a letter and use both first and second name:
Dear Mr Patrick Beavis or Dear Dr Susan Whitehouse

If you start a letter:
Dear Lover Boy or Dearest Snuffle Wuffle

You can write what you want at the end!

PS If you do write to your bank manager and start Dearest Snuffle Wuffle etc. you can write whatever you like but 'Yours faithfully' is probably too formal.
Also note that emails do not begin 'Dear Sir/Madam' but normally with the persons name.

BRAIN WORK Two: Quiz time

1. If a letter starts with Dear Mr Clinton it ends with ...?
2. If a letter ends with Yours faithfully it starts with ...?
3. If a letter starts with Dear Sir or Madam it ends with ...?
4. If you write a letter to somebody and you do not know their name or sex you start with ...?
5. If you write to Andreas Stecker, you start with ... and you end with ...? In this case be formal.

BRAIN WORK Three: Test your word power!

Put the correct word from the list below into the spaces in the letter.

dated	supply	note	understand
week	inferior	cancel	supplier

Dear Mr Hudson

Thank you very much for your letter ________ 20th November in which you say that you can ________ us with any spare parts for our taxis. We are happy to ________ that you can send these parts next ________.
We must point out that if the parts are of ________ quality we will be forced to ________ the order and find an alternative ________.
We are sure you ________ the situation.

Yours sincerely

A. Pacino

2 Chapter ENQUIRIES

Contents

Joke Time

The boss was interviewing[1] a young woman for the post[2] of secretary.
"How many words can you type a minute Miss Stevens?" he asked.
"Long words or short words?" she queried.[3]

A rather timid[4] office clerk came into Bob Onion's office.
"Excuse me, Mr Onion, I'm really sorry to bother[5] you right now, but you see I've been here five years now and my wife said it's time I was given a raise[6]. What do you think, Mr Onion?"
Bob Onion thought about this for a moment and then replied[7] "Well, I think it's fine by me but let me just check with my wife if you don't mind[8]."

1 Vorstellungsgespräch führen mit 2 Stelle 3 fragen 4 schüchtern 5 stören
6 Lohnerhöhung 7 antworten 8 nichts dagegen haben

FOCUS: Enquiries – an important first step

This type of letter is used to find customers, suppliers, agents and distributors. Most enquiries are short if the enquiry comes from buyers who want to place a limited order. However, if they want special conditions for regular orders or the right to sell for a producer the enquirers must try to sell the proposal.

The basic enquiry contains:

1) How you got the name of the potential supplier
2) The condition of the local market for the goods in question
3) What you want from the supplier, for example, catalogues, samples, price lists.

DIALOGUE: Introducing Onions

Onions is a British heating engineering company which produces boilers and other equipment. They are a small but growing company always interested in expanding. We will get to know some of the managers and other staff in their offices near Birmingham. Here we meet Ian Miller **(IM)** and Gerry Murry **(GM)** in the purchasing department.

IM: We need to reduce the costs of our units if we want to stay competitive.

GM: That's why I'm looking for other suppliers. Last month I was at a couple of trade fairs, one in Rome and another in Thailand.

IM: You certainly get about, Gerry. Did you get any contacts?

GM: Contacts, well, actually yes and no.

IM: I see, well, I was at a small trade fair near Bradford and I've seen one or two things in the press.

GM: Ha, Bradford, I haven't been there in years.

IM: No, you don't have time, I mean with all the work and travel.

GM: Yes, I know. Life can be very hard, it's true.

Drop Them A LINE: Enquiries to companies in Russia and Italy

Ian Miller and Gerry Murry write two letters:

Dear Sirs

We have seen your advertisement in 'The Engineer' and would appreciate it if you would kindly let us have details concerning your water pumps. Please send us a quotation for the items listed on the form enclosed. Give your prices CIF Hull. We would also like to know delivery times and terms of payment. In addition can you also indicate the types of discount you offer for regular and bulk orders.
If your prices are competitive and your products come up to our expectations we will be pleased to place substantial and regular orders.
We are looking forward to hearing from you soon

Yours faithfully

Ian Miller

Dear Sirs

We saw your pumps and other equipment demonstrated at the Mech-Tech engineering trade fair in Rome last month and would be grateful if you could send us information about your water pumps.
Will you kindly quote prices CIF Hull for the units on the enclosed list.
As well as this please inform us as to delivery times, terms of payment and sorts of discounts offered for regular and large orders.
If your prices are favourable and your products meet with our approval we will be happy to place large orders on a regular basis.
We would appreciate a prompt answer

Yours faithfully

Gerry Murry

Both letters ask for the same information but have different phrases to say the same thing. It is important to be able to say the same thing in different ways to avoid writing boring letters with limited flexibility of style.

VOCABULARY: To help you understand

actually	*eigentlich*
advertisement	*Annonce, Anzeige*
agent	*Vertreter*
appreciate	*zu schätzen wissen*
avoid	*vermeiden*
basic	*einfach*
boring	*langweilig*
bulk order	*Großauftrag*
buyer	*Käufer, Einkäufer*
catalogue	*Katalog*
CIF (Cost, Insurance, Freight)	*Kosten, Versicherung, Fracht*
come up to	*entsprechen*
competitive	*konkurrenzfähig*
concerning	*bezüglich*
contain	*enthalten*
customer	*Kunde*
delivery times	*Lieferzeiten*
discount	*Rabatt*
distributor	*Verteiler*
enclosed	*beiliegend*
enquirer	*Fragesteller/in*
enquiry	*Anfrage*
equipment	*Geräte, Ausrüstung*
expectations	*Erwartungen*
form	*Formular*
get to know	*kennen lernen*
heating engineering	*Heizungsinstallateur*
however	*jedoch*
in the press	*in der Presse*
indicate	*deuten auf*
item	*Artikel*
kindly	*freundlicherweise*
let us have	*schicken Sie uns*
limited	*beschränkt*
list	*auflisten*

local market	*örtlicher Markt*
look forward to	*sich freuen auf*
offer	*Angebot*
payment	*Zahlung*
place an order	*einen Auftrag erteilen*
post	*Stelle*
price list	*Preisliste*
proposal	*Vorschlag*
purchasing department	*Einkaufsabteilung*
quotation	*Kostenvoranschlag*
regular	*regelmäßig*
regular order	*regelmäßiger Auftrag*
right	*Recht*
sample	*Muster*
stay competitive	*konkurrenzfähig bleiben*
substantial	*wesentlich*
supplier	*Lieferant*
term	*Bedingung*
trade fair	*Messe*
unit	*Einheit*
water pumps	*Wasserpumpen*
you certainly get about	*Du kommst wirklich viel herum*

Put It ANOTHER WAY: Alternative phrases

Here are some phrases together with alternatives. Take a good look and check the meaning with the German.

would appreciate it	would be grateful	wären dankbar
kindly let us have	please send us	bitte schicken Sie uns
details concerning	information about	Informationen über
we would like to know	inform us as to	bitte teilen Sie uns mit
as well	in addition	auch

if your prices are favourable	if your prices are competitive	wenn Ihre Preise konkurrenzfähig sind
come up to our expectations	meet with our approval	unseren Erwartungen entsprechen
substantial	large	wesentlich
we are looking foward to hearing from you soon	we would appreciate a prompt answer*	wir freuen uns auf eine baldige Antwort

* "we would appreciate a prompt answer" sounds a little more formal than "we are looking forward to hearing from you"

BRAIN WORK One: What's the English for ...?

Here is your chance to do some work. Have a try at finding the English for the following sentences. The answers are in this chapter. Good luck!

1. Bitte teilen Sie uns mit
2. Wenn Ihre Preise konkurrenzfähig sind
3. Wenn Ihre Waren unseren Erwartungen entsprechen
4. Wir haben Ihre Anzeige in ... gesehen
5. Bitte machen Sie uns ein Angebot über

BRAIN WORK Two: Complete the letter

Please complete the following enquiry. The words you need are below. Use each word only once.

1. approval	**2.** in addition	**3.** competitive	**4.** grateful	**5.** concerning
6. terms	**7.** quotation	**8.** substantial	**9.** enclosed	

Dear Sirs

We saw your advertisement in last week's 'Gardening Now' and would be ... **(a)** ... if you would let us have information ... **(b)** ... your garden tools. Please send us a ... **(c)** ... for the items on the ... **(d)** ... list ... **(e)** ... we would also like to know delivery times, ... **(f)** ... of payment and the types of discount offered for ... (**g**) ... and regular orders. If your prices are ... (**h**) ... and the quality of your tools meets our ... (**i**) ... we will place a large order.

Yours faithfully

LETTER BOX: Using "would" and "could"

To make your letters more polite you should use verbs like *would* and *could*. In fact this makes letters sound both polite and more formal.

Send us details about your products clearly sounds rude.
Please send us ... is acceptable and polite enough but
Would you please send us ... is the usual form of request.

We want to have the goods next week would be OK to somebody you know but certainly not OK to a person you have never met. It sounds too direct.

We would like to have the goods next week is fine.
Could you please send us the goods next week? is more polite.

If you wish to sound even more polite and perhaps speculative:
Would it be possible for you to send the goods next week?

We were wondering if it might be possible for you to ...? This is asking for a favour and is very polite.

BRAIN WORK Three: Be polite!

Please make the following sentences polite. Use the examples in the Letter Box to help you.

Example: Give us information about your product.
Answer: Would / Could you please give us information about your product?

1. We want brochures about your tools.
2. Let us have your terms this week.

3. Tell us what types of discounts you offer.
4. Send us details about your wines and spirits.
5. Quote your prices CIF Melbourne.
6. We want delivery dates and discount details.

BRAIN WORK Four: Now you find the errors!

This is a good moment to practice your verbs and verb tenses! The following letter contains twelve errors. Find and correct them. A tip is look closely at the verbs. The key has notes on the answers.

Dear Mr Hudson

We visit your stand at the Birmingham Exhibition Centre last week. We is most interested in the discussion that we had with you and the brochures that we taking away with us.
We supplied hotel chains on the Spanish mainland and Balearic Islands with office furniture and we currently seek alternative suppliers.
We are also interested to note that you were having your own European transport department making delivery more accurate and quicker and that you could have delivered to us directly.
Please let us had a quotation for 35 office chairs type 'Manager' in blue cloth covering, 15 office desks Type T84 and 20 filing cabinets Type F18.
Additionally please informed us as to delivery times and terms of payment as well as types of discount offer for large and frequent orders.
If your prices is competitive and the delivery times, terms of payment and quality of products meet with our approval we will be happy to place substantial orders regularly.
We looking forward to a prompt response.

Yours sincerely

Phillip Sanchez

3 Chapter

OFFERS

Contents

Joke Time

We were introduced[1] to Onions in the last chapter. The boss of Onions, Bob Onion, wanted to promote[2] one of his junior managers to the senior executive[3] level. He handed out a questionnaire[4] to the possible candidates.
One of the questions was: Do you believe that you have executive potential?
One of the candidates wrote in answer: I think I have executive potential because I like to be alone, I never get lonely[5] and I would like to work in a private office on my own and I don't care[6] if people say bad things about me.

1 vorgestellt 2 befördern 3 Geschäftsleitung 4 Fragebogen 5 einsam 6 es ist mir egal

FOCUS: Offers – answering an enquiry

After the enquiry has been received the potential supplier will send the information (this could include catalogues, brochures, samples, details about prices, payment, delivery dates and discounts) requested.
The offer tells the customer that the seller is prepared to sell certain goods for a specific price and on certain conditions or terms.
There are unsolicited offers (a seller writes to a customer without an enquiry) and solicited offers (a seller writes in response to an enquiry).
The person submitting the offer may include all or some of the following:

1 There will be a time limit – there must be an acceptance in two, three weeks.

2 The offer may be without engagement – not legally binding.

3 Prices may be subject to change without notice.

4 Prices, delivery dates, terms of payment and delivery, quantity, type and quality of goods as well as details about any discounts.

DIALOGUE: Discussing offers

At the engineering company, Onions, Gerry Murry (**GM**) and Ian Miller (**IM**) are looking at the offers they received in reply to their letters.

IM: Take a look at these offers, Gerry. I think the offer from Russia is best.
GM: Really? Where is their factory? Moscow? Petersburg? Somebody might need to go out there and check things out. I've never been there, romantic places with cheap drink and food, I'll bet, vodka, champagne, caviar.
IM: Hmm, interesting you say that. I don't know if it's cheap but they probably have drink and food in Pomsk.
GM: Pomsk?! Where's that?
IM: Siberia, Central Siberia, not too far from Mongolia actually.
GM: Well, let's look at the offer from Rome and then the Russian one.

Drop Them A LINE: Receiving two offers

Ian Miller received a letter and Gerry Murry received a letter. Now have a look at both. Note the style and words used.

Dear Mr Miller

Many thanks for your enquiry dated 20th November. We appreciate your interest in our water pumps.
As requested we are sending you enclosed information about our products as well as delivery times, terms of payment and discounts.
By the same post we are also sending you samples of our water pumps.
The quantity discounts given in our price list vary depending on the size of the order. A cash discount is also allowed for payment within two months. Our prices are quoted CIF Hull.
Delivery can be effected on receipt of your order. This offer is valid for two weeks.
We are looking forward to hearing from you, and assure you that your order will receive immediate attention.

Yours sincerely
A. Popov

Dear Mr Murry

We are glad to learn from your letter of 20th November that you are interested in our pumps and we are pleased to send you a current price list together with our terms of business and details of our trade discounts.
We are sending you samples of our pumps by airmail.
If we receive your order before 1st January we will grant you an early order discount of 10%
This offer must be withdrawn after 14 days as demand for our products is high.
Please let us know your requirements soon

Yours faithfully
V. Antonini

VOCABULARY: To help you understand

acceptance	*Annahme*
allow	*gewähren*
appreciate	*gerne zur Kenntnis nehmen*
	zu schätzen wissen
assure	*versichern*
attention; your order will receive ~	*Ihre Bestellung wird bearbeitet*
bet	*wetten*
binding	*verbindlich*
brochure	*Prospekt*
by the same post	*mit gleicher Post*
cash discount	*Skonto*
catalogue	*Katalog*
certain	*bestimmt*
cheap	*billig*
conditions	*Bedingungen*
current	*aktuell*
delivery	*Lieferung*
delivery date	*Liefertermin*
depending on	*abhängig von*
discount	*Rabatt*
early order discount	*Frühdispositionsrabatt*
effect	*ausführen*
enquiry	*Anfrage*
factory	*Fabrik*
goods	*Waren*
immediate	*sofortig*
include	*einschließen*
offer	*Angebot*
on receipt	*nach Eingang*
prepared	*bereit*
probably	*wahrscheinlich*
quantity discount	*Mengenrabatt*
receive	*erhalten*
reply	*Antwort*

request	*bitten, Bitte*
requirement	*Bedarf*
response; in ~ to you enquiry	*in Beantwortung Ihrer Anfrage*
sample	*Muster*
seller	*Verkäufer*
size	*Größe*
solicit	*verlangen*
subject to change without notice	*Preisänderung vorbehalten*
submit	*einreichen, unterbreiten*
supplier	*Lieferant*
term	*Bedingung*
terms of payment	*Zahlungsbedingungen*
trade discount	*Händlerrabatt*
unsolicited	*unverlangt, nicht bestellt*
valid	*gültig*
withdraw an offer	*ein Angebot zurückziehen*
without engagement	*ohne Verpflichtung*

Put It ANOTHER WAY: Alternative phrases

To start a letter	
we were glad/pleased to receive your enquiry dated ...	wir haben uns über Ihre Anfrage vom ... gefreut
we refer to your enquiry of ...	wir beziehen uns auf Ihre Anfrage vom ...
we appreciate your interest in ...	wir freuen uns über Ihr Interesse an ...
as requested we are sending you ...	wunschgemäß, schicken wir Ihnen ...
Some terms and prices	
our prices are quoted ...	unsere Preise verstehen sich ...
our prices include packing and carriage	unsere Preise schließen Verpackung und Transport ein

transport and other charges to be borne by the purchaser	Transportkosten und andere Kosten zu Lasten des Käufers
we grant a discount of ... %	wir gewähren einen Rabatt von ... %

Some conditions

this offer is without engagement	dieses Angebot ist unverbindlich
this offer is firm / valid for ...	dieses Angebot ist ... gültig / fest für
all prices are subject to ...	alle Preise unterliegen ...
while stocks last	solange der Vorrat reicht

Ending a letter

we assure you that your order will be performed to your entire satisfaction	wir versichern Ihnen, dass Ihr Auftrag zu Ihrer vollen Zufriedenheit ausgeführt wird
you can rely on the careful execution of your order	Sie können sich auf die sorgfältige Ausführung Ihres Auftrages verlassen
we look forward to doing business with you	wir freuen uns darauf, mit Ihnen ins Geschäft zu kommen

BRAIN WORK One: Sort out the letter

You have had a hard day. You wrote a letter but it is mixed up.
The sentences are in the wrong order. Please sort out the problem.

- **a** Yours sincerely
- **b** Dear Mr Wilson
- **c** We look forward to the pleasure of doing business with you.
- **d** We were pleased to receive your enquiry dated ...
- **e** As requested we are sending you a catalogue and price list.
- **f** Please note that this offer and discount is valid for two weeks.
- **g** We are also pleased to grant you a discount of 10% for an early order.

BRAIN WORK Two: What's the English for ...?

And now more Brain Work. Over to you!
Use the glossary and vocabulary from the chapter to match the German to the English.

1. Solange der Vorrat reicht	**a** Our prices are quoted net
2. Wir danken Ihnen für Ihr Angebot	**b** We are willing to grant a special trade discount
3. Wir fügen unsere Preisliste bei	**c** Please note that
4. Unsere Preise verstehen sich netto	**d** We enclose our price-list
5. Wir sind bereit, einen Sonderhändlerrabatt zu gewähren	**e** While stocks last
6. Nehmen Sie bitte zur Kenntnis, dass	**f** We thank you for your offer

LETTER BOX: Short and long forms

In business and official letters you should not use short forms. For example:

We've received your offer	should be	*We have ...*
We're interested in your carpets		*We are ...*
I'm the manager of sales		*I am ...*
John'll write the letter		*John will ...*

Or:

She'd like to have a catalogue	*She would ...*
She'd quoted the price c.i.f.	*She had ...*
He's outside	*He is ...*
He's sent the fax	*He has ...*

The same with negatives:

We won't order the goods	should be	*We will not …*
We haven't sent the price-list		*We have not …*
It isn't valid		*It is not …*
He didn't receive the letter		*He did not …*

BRAIN WORK Three: Replace the short forms

This chapter was hard? Well, when you have done this little job have a rest! Use the Letter Box above to help you change the short forms and make the sentences formal.

1. We're sending you information as requested.
2. Your order'll receive immediate attention.
3. We'd like a special discount.
4. He didn't send the letter on Tuesday.
5. It's very expensive.
6. The firm hasn't granted a discount.

BRAIN WORK Four: A little puzzle with vocabulary

Here are some words from this chapter but they are mixed up. To help you there are also some German words below. What are the English words and what is the German word for them?

1. sperupli
2. curbhore
3. galocatue
4. feofr
5. qrestue
6. amples

Katalog, Lieferant, Muster, Prospekt, Bitte, Angebot

4 Chapter

ORDERS

ORDERS

Contents

FOCUS: Orders – accepting an offer
DIALOGUE: Discussing the placement of an order
DROP THEM A LINE: An order to the Russians
PUT IT ANOTHER WAY: Alternative phrases
BRAIN WORK: Sort out a letter and some tests

Joke Time

At Onions a clerk[1] goes in to see Bob Onion.

Clerk: Excuse me, Mr Onion but I've been here now fifteen years and that means fifteen years of experience[2]. I think it's time I had a rise[3].

Onion: That's not fifteen years of experience. You see, you've had one year of experience fifteen times.

1 Büroangestellte/r 2 Erfahrung 3 Gehaltserhöhung

FOCUS: Orders – accepting an offer

If the offer from the seller is acceptable to the buyer he or she will place an order. Sometimes a firm will send a special order form, at other times orders are placed over the phone. However, an order should be confirmed in writing if it is placed over the phone. If an order form is sent, a covering letter should be enclosed because it makes clear and confirms agreed conditions such as delivery dates and discounts.

DIALOGUE: Discussing the placement of an order

Gerry Murry (**GM**) and Ian Miller (**IM**) are discussing an order for water pumps with Bob Onion (**BO**).

BO: So what do you think, the Russian pumps, cheaper but more risky or place an order for the Italian pumps?
GM: I think the Italian company would be better, the samples were better quality.
IM: Yes, but the Russian pumps were good enough for what we need. What's more they are 30% cheaper for large orders. We could place other orders for pipes and cables with Popov's if this order is okay.
BO: Good thinking, Ian. That's what I like to see, enterprising positive thinking! Let's place an order with these Russians.
IM: Right, I'll write a letter straight away.

Drop Them A LINE: An order to the Russians

So, after the meeting Ian writes to Popov's:

Dear Mr. Popov

Thank you for your quotation and terms of ... as well as the sample pump.
We have tested your product and are pleased to place the following order for 400 water pumps type T82B.
For your information we have instructed our bank here in Birmingham to

open an irrevocable letter of credit in your favour payable at the International Trade Bank in Pomsk.
The sales conditions are as follows:

Price:	£25.50 per pump
Packing:	cases lined with styrofoam
Payment:	irrevocable letter of credit
Delivery:	by 1st May at the latest in Liverpool

We must point out that the quality must correspond to the sample supplied. If this order is completed to our satisfaction we will place regular orders with your firm.

Yours sincerely

Ian Miller
Chief Buyer

VOCABULARY: To help you understand

accept	*annehmen*
agreed condition	*vereinbarte Bedingung*
as well as	*sowie*
at the latest	*spätestens*
buyer	*Käufer*
case	*Kiste*
clerk	*Büroangestellte*
complete	*ausführen*
condition	*Bedingung*
confirm	*bestätigen*
correspond	*entsprechen*
covering letter	*Begleitbrief*
delivery date	*Liefertermin*
discount	*Rabatt*
enclose	*beilegen*
enterprising	*unternehmungslustig*
experience	*Erfahrung*
following	*folgende*

for your information	*zu Ihrer Information*
however	*jedoch*
in writing	*schriftlich*
in your favour	*zu Ihren Gunsten*
instruct	*anweisen*
irrevocable letter of credit	*unwiderrufliches Akkreditiv*
lined with styrofoam	*mit Schaumstoff ausgekleidet*
order	*Auftrag*
order form	*Bestell-Formular*
payable	*zahlbar*
pipe	*Rohr*
place an order	*Auftrag erteilen*
pleased to	*sich freuen, etwas zu tun*
point out	*hinweisen auf*
quotation	*Preisangabe*
raise	*Gehaltserhöhung*
regular / regularly	*regelmäßig*
risky	*riskant*
sales condition	*Verkaufsbedingung*
sample	*Muster*
term	*Bedingung*
to our satisfaction	*zu unser Zufriedenheit*
what's more	*außerdem*

Put It ANOTHER WAY: Alternative phrases

To start	
we were pleased to receive...	wir haben uns gefreut ... zu bekommen
many thanks for ...	vielen Dank für ...
please let us have ...	bitte senden Sie uns ...
kindly supply ...	bitte liefern Sie ...

Conditions	
please arrange early delivery	bitte sorgen Sie für baldige Lieferung
I look forward to receiving ... within ... days	ich freue mich darauf, ... zu erhalten innerhalb ... Tagen
please advise / notify us	bitte teilen Sie uns mit
as soon as the goods are shipped	sobald die Waren abgesandt worden sind
please despatch the goods by rail	bitte senden Sie die Waren mit der Bahn
Ending the letter	
we request / ask that you give this order prompt attention	wir bitten Sie, diesen Auftrag sofort zu erledigen
we shall place further orders with you if this order is satisfactorily executed	wir werden Ihnen weitere Aufträge erteilen, wenn dieser Auftrag zufriedenstellend ausgeführt wird

BRAIN WORK One: Sort out a letter

Time for you to do a bit of work. Please put the following parts of a letter in the correct order. Don't forget to use the alternative phrases in above.

1.	a	Yours sincerely
2.	b	We shall place further orders with you if this order is satisfactorily executed
3.	c	We were pleased to receive your quotation of 12th May
4.	d	Kindly supply us with five kilos of first quality English Tea
5.	e	Please arrange an early delivery and notify us as soon as the goods are shipped
6.	f	Dear Mrs. Jackson

BRAIN WORK Two: What's the English for ...?

Here is a nice simple job for you to do. Have fun! Please put the English word with the German word.

1. condition	a Muster
2. in writing	b einen Auftrag erteilen
3. place an order	c Bedingung
4. enclose	d bestätigen
5. sample	f schriftlich
6. confirm	g beilegen

BRAIN WORK Three: Put in the right words

How do you feel? Just a bit more Brain Work.
Please put the following words in the sentences. Use each word once.

payable quotation place point satisfaction irrevocable

1. The letter of credit is ... at your local bank.
2. Thank you for your ... and terms of delivery.
3. I ought to ... out that the quality of the product must be good.
4. We are pleased to ... the following order.
5. We will open an ... letter of credit.
6. If the products are to our ... we will place more orders.

BRAIN WORK Four: See if you see the mistake

Each of these sentences contains one mistake. Find the mistake and correct it.

1. We are very peased to receive your quotation.
2. We will plaice further orders with you.
3. We will order more bags from you if they good quality are.
4. I look forward to receive the samples.
5. Thank you for the informations about the motor.
6. I has tested the product and am happy to send an order.

5 Chapter ACKNOWLEDGEMENTS

Contents

FOCUS: Acknowledging an order
DIALOGUE: The Russians wonder how to acknowledge Onions' order
DROP THEM A LINE: A correct acknowledgement
PUT IT ANOTHER WAY: Alternative phrases
BRAIN WORK: Test yourself and your memory!

Joke Time

A few years ago Bob Onion was interviewed by a journalist from a local newspaper about the success[1] of the company.
The journalist asked Bob: "How do you find easy answers to problems in the area of production?"
Bob thought for a moment and said: "Normally we hand[2] the problem to the laziest person in the factory. They will find the easiest way to deal with the problem and then we simply use their method."

1 Erfolg 2 weiter-/übergeben

FOCUS: Acknowledging an order

In foreign trade it is normal to send the buyer a written acknowledgement because it can take the goods some time to arrive. Often the seller cannot supply the goods – goods not available from stock – or the seller does not accept the customer's conditions because the discounts or prices are not acceptable. In such cases the seller will usually put forward alternatives, perhaps suggesting a different product or different conditions. This is called a counter-offer.

DIALOGUE: The Russians wonder how to acknowledge Onions' order

In Pomsk Alex Popov (**AP**) and Vladimir Oblomov (**VO**), owners of a small engineering factory, are very happy. As we know they have received an order from Onions in Birmingham for water pumps. Here they are talking to Alex Mitchel (**AM**), a visiting businessman from Scotland about further business.

AP: Well, Mr Mitchel, our products are selling well in Europe.

AM: Really? That's good news. That's why I'm here too. Maybe we can come to an agreement for distributing your equipment in Britain. My firm could act as your agent and we would deal with all advertising and correspondence.

VO: Correspondence? Oh yes, you mean this letter writing. A big problem for us. We are engineers, not language specialists. And we are not sure about the way you do things. For example, we have an order by post. Is it normal to tell the customer you are dealing with the order? And how? I mean to write and inform them that the order is being produced and when it will be sent? Should you say "Your conditions of business are fine"?

AM: Absolutely. You should tell them you accept the terms ...

AP: Terms?

AM: That means conditions. You should also tell them the goods will arrive on time. You should say things like "We are giving your order priority" and start "Thank you for your order dated ..."

AP: Wonderful. Vladimir, do you have a pen and paper and Mr. Mitchel, do you have perhaps five minutes?

Drop Them A LINE: A correct acknowledgement

So, after about ten minutes Alex wrote a letter for the Russians to Onions. Here is the letter:

Dear Mr Miller

Thank you very much for your order no. 2493F dated ... for 400 water pumps type T82B. We accept your order at the prices given in your letter as well as the other conditions.
We can confirm that we have sufficient pumps of this type in stock and that the delivery date can be met. As soon as our bank advises us that payment has been arranged, we will organise shipment of the consignment by MS Argus sailing on 12th April from Petersburg due to arrive on 20th April in Liverpool.
We hope that this will be the beginning of a long and successful business relationship and we look forward to hearing from you again soon.

Yours sincerely

A. Popov

VOCABULARY: To help you understand

acknowledgement	*Auftragsbestätigung*
advertise	*Werbung machen*
advise	*(hier) informieren*
agent	*Vertreter*
area	*Gebiet*
arrive	*ankommen*
as soon as	*so bald wie*
available	*vorrätig, lieferbar*
buyer	*Käufer*
case	*Fall*
consignment	*Lieferung, Sendung*
counter-offer	*Gegenangebot*
deal with	*fertig werden mit, verhandeln mit*

delivery date	*Liefertermin*
distribute	*verteilen*
due; the goods are ~ to arrive on the ...	*die Waren sollen eintreffen/ sind fällig am ...*
equipment	*Ausrüstung, Geräte*
foreign trade	*Außenhandel*
further	*weiter*
lazy	*faul*
look forward to	*sich auf etwas freuen*
meet; ~ a date	*einen Termin einhalten*
owner	*Besitzer*
payment	*Zahlung*
priority	*Vorrang*
put forward	*vorschlagen*
relationship	*Beziehung*
sail	*abfahren*
shipment	*Sendung, Verschiffung*
stock (from stock)	*Vorrat (ab Lager)*
success	*Erfolg*
successful	*erfolgreich*
sufficient	*ausreichend*
suggest	*vorschlagen*
term	*Bedingung*

Put It ANOTHER WAY: Alternative phrases

To start	
we thank you for your order placed on ...	wir danken Ihnen für Ihren Auftrag vom ...
many thanks for your order	vielen Dank für Ihren Auftrag
Other details	
your goods will be sent/despatched within a few days	Ihre Waren werden in wenigen Tagen abgesandt werden

we will do our best/utmost to complete your order in good time	wir werden uns sehr bemühen, Ihren Auftrag rechtzeitig zu erfüllen
we regret that we cannot supply the goods you ordered	wir bedauern, dass wir nicht in der Lage sind, die von Ihnen bestellten Waren zu liefern
unfortunately we no longer stock this item	leider führen wir diesen Artikel nicht mehr
Ending the letter	
we feel certain that you will be satisfied with ...	wir sind sicher, dass Sie mit ... zufrieden sein werden
we hope that this will be the first of many orders	wir hoffen, dass dies der Erste von vielen Aufträgen sein wird

BRAIN WORK One: What's the English for ...?

Okay, over to you. Have a try at the little brain tests that follow.
Here are some English and German words and phrases from this chapter.
Put the words together.

1. unfortunately	**a** einen Artikel führen
2. we feel certain	**b** wir bedauern, dass
3. stock an item	**c** in wenigen Tagen
4. we will do our utmost	**d** rechtzeitig
5. we regret that	**e** wir werden uns sehr bemühen
6. in good time	**f** leider
7. within a few days	**g** wir sind sicher

BRAIN WORK Two: Put in the missing letters

Here are some words but the secretary was a bit sleepy and missed out a few letters. Your job: identify the words and put in the missing letters.

1. s-ff-ci-nt	**2.** a-v-se	**3.** p-y-en-
4. c-nsi-nm-n-	**5.** s-cce-s-ul	**6.** d-li-er-

BRAIN WORK Three: Complete the letter

Oh dear, the secretary was sleepy! Below is a letter with some words missing. To make it a little easier the missing words are in the box. Use the words below (1 to 8) once to make the letter acceptable.

1. to hearing	**2.** despatch	**3.** many thanks for	**4.** regret
5. dated	**6.** item	**7.** within	**8.** no longer

Dear Sir

... (**a**) ... your order number A251... (**b**) ... 25th September 03 for 240 pull-overs and 180 sweatshirts.
We... (**c**) ... that we cannot supply the sweatshirts because we ... (**d**) ... stock this ... (**e**) ... We will ... (**f**) ... the pullovers ... (**g**) ... 5 days and look forward ... (**h**) ... from you again soon.

Yours faithfully

BRAIN WORK Four: You construct a good letter

Make a good letter from the mixed up sentences.

1. We are certain that this is the start of a successful business relationship.
2. We are happy to accept the order at the price stated by you along with your other terms.
3. Shipment will be organised as soon as our bank advises us that payment arranged.
4. The consignment will be shipped on MS Nostromo sailing from Lisbon 21st May and due to arrive on 29th May in Port Elizabeth.
5. We have sufficient cabinets in stock and can deliver by the date given.
6. We look forward to hearing from you in the near future.
7. We wish to thank you for your order no. 55729 for office 257 filing cabinets type F18.

6 Chapter SUPPLY PROBLEMS

SUPPLY PROBLEMS

Contents

FOCUS: Problems with supply and delivery
DIALOGUE: Strikes and trouble for Onions
DROP THEM A LINE: Delivery time cannot be met
PUT IT ANOTHER WAY: Alternative phrases
BRAIN WORK: Understanding and constructing letters

Joke Time

Bob Onion was visiting Gerry Murry who was in hospital with a broken leg[1]. Onion said: "Don't worry[2] Gerry, everybody at work is ready to cover for[3] you while you are off work."
"Oh, that's good!" said Gerry.
"Yes, as soon as we know what you have been doing!"

1 gebrochenes Bein 2 keine Sorge 3 einspringen

FOCUS: Problems with supply and delivery

When buyer and supplier have agreed on conditions the supplier then must deliver the goods. The delivery is usually organised by the seller. Small, light items can be sent by post. For larger orders a forwarding agent is normally used. Often the buyer will ask for a despatch advice which says when the goods have been shipped. There are many reasons why an order cannot be executed. In this case a supplier should inform the buyer of the reasons for a delay or other problems.

DIALOGUE: Strikes and troubles for Onions

At Onions there have been one or two problems in the factory. The union has decided that overtime on Sundays should be double normal pay. At the moment Onions is very successful and the order books are so full that the factory is working at full capacity, and to execute all orders for heating equipment there is work on Saturdays and Sundays.
Ian Burns (**IB**), the new head of personnel is talking to the shop steward, Mick Lake (**ML**).

ML: Business is very good. We are doing a lot of overtime at the moment and we want more pay for it.

IB: Yes, but we must be competitive. Look at those other firms that have not cut their costs. They have gone bankrupt. No job at all!

ML: Well, if you don't offer more money I'm afraid we'll work to rule and there may be a go slow.

IB: What, industrial action? We will lose orders and you'll lose jobs.

ML: The members of the union have decided to take industrial action until Onions sees reason!

Later Ian Burns talks to Bob Onion (**BO**).

BO: So it looks like we'll have delays in orders and perhaps some cancellations. Damn it Burns, we Onions have sold boilers for years and never had any trouble with unions. Onions and unions have never had problems. That is until I hired university types and had a personnel department!

IB: At the moment the union is not doing overtime. It will clearly hold up orders.

BO: Do something, Burns! Fire somebody, that's what I pay you for!

IB: It just isn't as simple as that. We'll have to tell our customers that we have problems. A few letters must be written.

BO: If this goes on much longer you will be writing a few letters, letters of application!

Drop Them A LINE: Delivery time cannot be met

We have seen that Onions have got production problems. Here is one of a lot of letters sent out that week to customers:

Dear Sir

We very much regret to inform you that we are forced to ask for an extension of time in the execution of your order no. E560 placed on 16th March. Industrial action at our plant in Birmingham has resulted in a delay in despatching some orders. However, we believe that we can carry out delivery within a week. We apologise for the delay and hope you have understanding for our difficulties and please be assured that we are doing all we can to make the delivery on time.
As you requested we will advise you as soon as the order is ready for shipment.

Yours faithfully

VOCABULARY: To help you understand

apologise	*sich entschuldigen*
assure somebody	*jemandem versichern*
buyer	*Käufer*
cancellation	*Stornierung*
carry out	*ausführen*
competitive	*konkurrenzfähig*
cover for	*einspringen für*
cut the costs	*die Kosten reduzieren*
delay	*Verspätung*
delivery time	*Lieferzeit*
despatch	*senden*
despatch advice	*Versandanzeige*
don't worry	*keine Sorge*
execute orders	*Bestellungen ausführen*
execution	*Ausführung*
extension	*Verlängerung*
force; ~ somebody to do something	*jemanden zwingen, etwas zu tun*
forwarding agent	*Spediteur*
go slow	*Bummelstreik*
goods	*Waren*
hold up	*verspäten, Verspätung*
in this case	*in diesem Fall*
industrial action	*Arbeitskampfmaßnahmen*
order book	*Auftragsbuch*
overtime	*Überstunden*
plant	*Fabrik*
reason	*Vernunft, Grund*
request	*bitten, ersuchen*
result in	*führen zu*
ship	*versenden, verschiffen*
shop steward	*Arbeitnehmervertreter*
union	*Gewerkschaft*
work to rule	*Dienst nach Vorschrift*

Put It ANOTHER WAY: Alternative phrases

To start	
we are really/indeed sorry	wir bedauern wirklich
please accept our apologies for	bitte nehmen Sie unsere Entschuldigung entgegen
we regret to have to tell you that ...	wir bedauern, Ihnen mitteilen zu müssen, dass ...
Reasons for the delay	
demand was so great that ...	Nachfrage war so groß, dass ...
our stock has been exhausted/used up	unsere Vorräte sind erschöpft
a fire damaged our plant	ein Feuer hat unsere Fabrik beschädigt
our suppliers found it impossible to keep pace with orders	unsere Lieferanten waren nicht imstande, mit den Aufträgen Schritt zu halten
an unexpected shortage of raw materials	eine unerwartete Rohstoffknapp-heit
Ending the letter	
we hope that you will appreciate/understand our position	wir hoffen, dass Sie unsere Lage verstehen
we hope that this delay will not cause you considerable inconvenience	wir hoffen, dass diese Verzögerung Ihnen keine wesentlichen Unannehmlichkeiten verursacht
we wish to assure that we are doing everything to despatch your order	wir möchten Ihnen versichern, dass wir alles tun, Ihren Auftrag auf den Weg zu bringen

BRAIN WORK One: A little letter writing

This time please put the words below into the letter.

despatch assure position damaged delay sorry executing

Dear Mrs Duffy

We are really ... (1) ... to inform you that there will be a delay in ... (2) ... your order number F1644 placed on 1st June of this year.
The reason for the ... (3) ... is that a fire ... (4) .... our factory last week.
We hope you understand our ... (5) ... and we wish to ... (6) ... you that we are doing everything to ... (7) ... your order within 14 days.

Yours sincerely

R. Ahonen

BRAIN WORK Two: Quiz time

Okay, let's see what you can remember. Ready? Good luck!
Circle one letter for the correct answer.

1. "A cancellation of an order" means:
- **a** the order will be late
- **b** the order will be early
- **c** there will be no order

2. "Despatch an order" means:
- **a** to send the order
- **b** to put the order in boxes
- **c** to repair the goods

3. A "plant" is another word for:
- **a** a factory
- **b** a sort of office
- **c** a sort of strike

4. "The strike will hold up delivery" means:
- **a** delivery will be by air
- **b** delivery will be late
- **c** delivery will be sent now

5. "To apologise" means:
- **a** to say hello
- **b** to say sorry
- **c** to deliver

6. "To request" is another way to say:
- **a** to ask for
- **b** to do again
- **c** to carry out

BRAIN WORK Three: How much do you understand?

Read the letter below then answer the questions.

We sincerely apologise for the inconvenience caused you by the delay in delivery of 15 days for our four forklift trucks (*Gabelstapler*). Production was set back slightly (*leicht aufgehalten worden*) by the late arrival or some components which was caused by the breakdown of a machine at our supplier's plant. This is the first time in that production has been held up for this reason. Additionally orders have been rather heavy over recent months but we assure you that we are making every effort to get the vehicles to in the next two days. Once again we regret very much having given you cause for complaint and wish to stress that such a delay will not be repeated in future.
Yours sincerely

1. How long is the delay?
2. What has been delayed?
3. Find a phrase that means 'we are very sorry for the problems created'.
4. What broke down?
5. Give two phrases in English from the letter that mean 'aufhalten'.
6. What two reasons are given for the delay?
7. Find a word in the letter that means 'also' and 'factory'.
8. What does 'stress' mean here in German?

BRAIN WORK Four: You construct a letter

Here are a number of parts of sentences. Put them together in order to make a good letter.

1. the delay in delivery of 5 days
2. this was due to production problems
3. Dear Mr Hudson we sincerely regret
4. within the next two days
5. and the inconvenience caused you
6. and will reach you
7. the goods have already been despatched
8. Yours sincerely J Woodward
9. at our supplier's plant

PAYMENT

Chapter 7

Contents

Joke Time

Bob Onion decided to hire a chauffeur from an agency to drive his Rolls. On the first morning Bob Onion asked him "Driver, what's your name?"
"George, sir," replied the chauffeur.
"I don't call my drivers by their first name! What's your second name?"
"Well, it's Darling, sir."
"In that case, drive on George," said Onion.

FOCUS: How to pay bills abroad

Paying for products at home is a simple matter. We can pay in advance or after delivery. Payment is normally by cheque, draft or transfer. There can be problems if the buyer does not want to or cannot pay.
In foreign trade these problems are greater. There is a lot of correspondence and the seller must wait months for payment, the buyer must wait months for the goods. Banks are very important here because they help to collect payment, handle shipping documents and act as agents for foreign banks. They also guarantee conditions of payment. Payment for foreign trade is usually made by banker's transfer, letter of credit or bill of exchange.

DIALOGUE: The head of sales learns a few things

Tom Parker (**TP**) is the head of sales at Onions. He is talking to Sally Benson (**SB**) in finance about paying customers abroad and more important about being paid.

TP: You see Sally, I've been with Onions for 20 years. Most of the time we've done business with companies in Britain, we've hardly sold anything abroad, you know, to foreign companies.

SB: Things change, Tom. We must be flexible and we need to expand. We must sell and buy outside Britain if we want to stay in business.

TP: It's all so complicated. I mean in Britain, for example, if I wanted parts from Potters Ltd, I just wrote them a cheque or transferred the money to their account. Simple, no problem.

SB: Yes, but you can't do that with a company 5,000 miles away, maybe in India. Sellers can't be sure they'll get their money and buyers can't be sure they'll get their goods.

TP: That's the problem! Precisely.

SB: It's not a problem if, for example, you use a letter of credit. Let's say that we want to buy components worth £500 from a company in Korea. We ask our bank to issue a letter of credit for £500 in favour of the seller. There is a special form for this. It contains all the conditions of the transaction agreed by us and the firm in Korea. Then, our bank sends these instructions to its agent in Korea. In this case the agent is a bank. The bank in Korea contacts the sellers and advises them of the credit. Now this is very safe.

TP: Why's that?

SB: Because the agent bank will pay the sellers if the conditions on the letter are fulfilled, so the sellers can execute our order and know they will be paid. We are happy because the agent bank only pays if we get our goods according to the order.

TP: I'm still not totally clear ...

SB: Look at these letters ...

Drop Them A LINE: Arranging payment

Here is a letter written to Onions by Arumco in Saudi Arabia with an order for special industrial heating units for a chemical process.

Dear Sirs

Thank you for your letter dated 18th March 20.. enclosing your terms and catalogue. We wish to place the attached order and would appreciate prompt execution.
We have instructed The El Turkiy National Bank Damman to open a credit for £8,540 in your favour, valid until 30th June 20.. . The credit will be confirmed by their agent bank The G.I.F. Bank, 27 Booker street, Birmingham T48SOW who will accept your draft on them for the amount of your invoice for 60 days.
Please attach the following documents to your draft:

Insurance policy for £9,000
2 commercial invoices
2 bills of lading

Please advise us when the units have been despatched.

Yours faithfully

Mohamed Al Baab

Onions sent a reply to the above letter:

Dear Mr Al Baab

We were very happy to receive your order and can confirm that the units you request are in stock.
We agree to your method of payment and note that it is by irrevocable letter of credit for a sum not in excess of £8,540 valid until 30th June 20..
As soon as we receive confirmation of this credit from The G.I.F. Bank in Birmingham, we shall despatch your order.
We assure you that your order is being given prompt attention and that the units ordered by you are of the best quality.

Yours sincerely

Frank Howard

VOCABULARY: To help you understand

abroad	*im Ausland*
accept a draft	*einen Wechsel akzeptieren*
according to	*entsprechend*
act as an agent	*als Agent arbeiten*
advance; in ~	*im voraus*
advise	*benachrichtigen*
agency	*Agentur*
amount	*Betrag*
attach	*beiheften*
bill	*Rechnung*
bill of exchange	*übertragbare Zahlungsanweisung, Wechsel*
bill of lading	*Seefrachtbrief/Konnossement*
collect payment	*einziehen, Inkasso durchführen*
commercial invoice	*Handelsrechnung*
condition of payment	*Zahlungsbedingung*
confirm	*bestätigen*
contain	*enthalten*
darling	*Schatz, Liebling*

decide	*entscheiden; sich ~*
draft	*Tratte, gezogener Wechsel*
excess; in ~ of	*übersteigen, hinausgehen über*
execute	*ausführen*
execution	*Ausführung*
favour; in your favour ~	*zu Ihren Gunsten*
foreign trade	*Außenhandel*
form	*Formular*
fulfil	*erfüllen*
handle	*bearbeiten*
head	*Leiter*
instruct, instruction	*anweisen, Anweisung*
insurance policy	*Versicherungspolice*
invoice	*Warenrechnung*
irrevocable letter of credit	*unwiderrufliches Akkreditiv*
issue a letter of credit	*ein Akkreditiv ausstellen*
letter of credit	*Akkreditiv, Kreditbrief*
matter	*Sache*
note	*zur Kenntnis nehmen*
shipping documents	*Versanddokumente*
transaction	*Geschäft, Transaktion, Abwicklung*
transfer	*überweisen, Überweisung*
valid until	*gültig bis*

Put It ANOTHER WAY: Alternative phrases

we have arranged payment through the N.I.T. Bank for the amount of ...	wir haben Zahlung in Höhe von ... durch die N.I.T. Bank vorgenommen
we have transferred the amount to your account	wir haben auf Ihr Konto den Betrag überwiesen
cash on delivery/COD	per Nachnahme
cash in advance	Vorauszahlung

I thank you for your delivery and I enclose a cheque covering the amount of your invoice.	ich danke Ihnen für Ihre Lieferung und füge einen Scheck über den Rechnungsbetrag bei
the goods arrived in good condition	die Waren sind in gutem Zustand angekommen

BRAIN WORK One: Complete the sentences

Test yourself a little more and please complete these sentences with the words below. Use each word once. Use the first letter in this chapter to help you. Please note, there is an extra word!

confirmed valid execute favour instructed attach

1. Please ... shipping documents
2. We have ... our bank in Tobago to open a letter of credit in your ...
3. Please ... the order promptly.
4. The credit is ... until 15th April 20.. .
5. The letter of credit will be ... by their agent bank in Stockholm.

BRAIN WORK Two: True or false?

This is another bit of brain work but see how you do and then have a rest! From the text on payment decide which of the statements below are true or false.

	T	F
1. It is more complex paying for products at home.		
2. Sellers must wait longer for payment with foreign trade.		
3. Banks are important in foreign trade.		
4. Bills of exchange and letters of credit are not used in foreign trade.		

BRAIN WORK Three: Letter writing

Your chance to use what you have learned in this chapter! Here is a letter discussing payment. Please put in the words below to complete the letter.

confirmed enclosing instructed agent valid irrevocable open

Dear Sir

Many thanks for your letter of 20th June 19.. ... (1) ... your terms and information about the radios and television sets produced by your firm. We wish to place an order.

We have ... (2) ... our bank, The International Finance Bank Durban, to ... (3) ... an ... (4) ... letter of credit for US$ 1,850 in your favour ... (5) ... until 20th September. The credit will be ... (6) ... by their ... (7) ... bank in London,
The PLS Bank, 32 Queensbury rd., LONDON SW4 3G1 who will accept your draft on them for the amount of your invoice.

Yours faithfully

BRAIN WORK Four: Put the sentences in order

Here are six typical sentences from letters about payment. Please put the words in the correct order.

1. to inform we wish you that arranged payment we have the Royal Dutch Bank the of amount $120,000 through for
2. we will the £380 please note that transfer your account next Friday to
3. our cash on terms are delivery
4. all items to inform you that arrived in good condition I am pleased
5. covering I enclose a your bill cheque the amount of
6. will despatch as payment as soon is made we order your

BRAIN WORK Five: How much do you understand?

Read the two letters below then answer the questions.

Letter One

Dear Mr Hudson

The consignment of machine parts arrived yesterday of which you informed us on April 11th. We have examined the items and we have found them to be in order.

We will pay your invoice by bank transfer as arranged to your account with the HDF bank in Baghdad.

We would appreciate it if you would confirm payment by email or fax as soon as possible.

Yours sincerely

Letter Two

Dear Mr Masembe

I wish to thank you for the prompt shipment of the six crates of wooden ornaments we requested last week.

We received them earlier today and having examined them we have found that they are in order.

In payment of your invoice we are sending a cheque for £4,760 to your bank here in England (The Bank of Kenya) as arranged.

We would be grateful if you could confirm that you are in receipt of payment as soon as you can preferably by telephone.

Yours sincerely

Questions

1. Letter One and Letter Two use different words for delivery, what are these words?
2. How is payment to be made in the two letters?
3. Why are telephone, fax and email mentioned?
4. Both letters say that the writer 'zu schätzen wissen' but how in English?
5. What word or words are used in the letters to say 'we have looked at the goods'?
6. What happened on April 11th?
7. How do the writers say in English 'in gutem Zustand'?

Chapter 8

DELAYS IN PAYMENT, PART ONE

Contents

FOCUS: Delays in payment – asking for your money!
DIALOGUE: A telephone call to ask about payment
DROP THEM A LINE: A follow-up to the phone call
PUT IT ANOTHER WAY: Alternative phrases
BRAIN WORK: Correcting a letter and some tests

Joke Time

A customer phones Gerry Murry's secretary in the sales department at Onions.

Customer: I'd like to talk to Mr Murry, please.
Secretary: I'm very sorry but he's not in this afternoon.
Customer: Well, this is the third time I've tried to reach him! Doesn't he work in the afternoon?
Secretary: Oh no, you are wrong. Actually he doesn't work in the morning. He just doesn't come in the office in the afternoon.

FOCUS: Delays in payment – asking for your money!

Sometimes a customer will not pay on time. In this case you should not think that she or he does not intend to pay. There could be a number of reasons why the account is overdue. Perhaps the customer did not receive your bill or the bill has been overlooked. Maybe there has been a problem with payment, a lost cheque in the post, a misunderstanding at the bank. So the first letter should be a polite enquiry asking about the delay. If the customer ignores the first letter or acknowledges it but still does not pay you should write a second letter. This letter should be a little more firm. You should refer to the previous letter and send copies of relevant bills. The third request or final demand should review the situation so far, saying you have been patient, and telling the customer what action you will take. Do not threaten legal action unless you intend to take it!

DIALOGUE: A telephone call to ask about payment

Susan Wright (**SW**), a member of the sales department at Onions, telephones a building company to ask why they have not paid a bill for heating equipment (**S: secretary**).

S: Hello, Melmoths the builders. Can I help you?

SW: Good morning, my name is Susan Wright and I'm phoning about some heating equipment your firm ordered from us two months ago. Can I speak to Mr Melmoth, please?

S: Oh, er, he's away at the moment.

SW: Will he be away long?

S: I'm not sure actually, you see he's been rather ill and ...

SW: Well, maybe you could help.You see we haven't been paid for ...

S: Oh, I don't think I can help you there. I'm only temporary, standing in and answering the phone. Could you write a letter and I'll see that Mr Melmoth gets it?

SW: Well, okay. You'll get the letter in a few days.

Drop Them A LINE: A follow-up to the phone call

The golden rule is always to have something on paper!
So after the telephone conversation Susan Wright writes a letter to Melmoths reminding the firm about the overdue bill:

Dear Mr Melmoth

As you normally clear your accounts promptly we think you may have overlooked our invoice No 7D 34 for £453.75 which was due six weeks ago. Could you please let us have your cheque to clear the bill? However, if you have already sent a remittance, please disregard this letter.
Attached please find a copy of the bill.
We look forward to hearing from you soon.

Yours sincerely

VOCABULARY: To help you understand

account	*Rechnung, Konto*
acknowledgement	*Bestätigung*
attached	*beigeheftet, beiliegend*
builder	*Bauunternehmer*
clear a bill	*begleichen; eine Rechnung ~*
delay	*Verspätung, Verzögerung*
disregard	*ignorieren, nicht beachten*
due	*fällig*
enquiry	*Anfrage*
final demand	*letzte Mahnung*
firm	*bestimmt, fest*
heating equipment	*Heizgerät*
intend	*beabsichtigen*
invoice	*Warenrechnung*
legal action	*Klage*
member	*Mitglied*

misunderstanding	*Missverständnis*
on time	*pünktlich*
overdue	*überfällig*
overlook	*übersehen*
previous	*vorhergehend, früher*
reason	*Grund*
refer to	*sich beziehen auf*
remind somebody of	*erinnern; jemanden ~ an*
remittance	*Zahlung*
request	*Bitte*
settle a bill	*ausgleichen, begleichen*
settlement	*Bezahlung, Übertragung*
stand in	*einspringen, vertreten*
temporary	*vorübergehend*
threaten	*drohen*

Put It ANOTHER WAY: Alternative phrases

Starting a letter	
we should like to remind you that ...	wir möchten Sie daran erinnern, dass ...
we are sorry to inform you that...	es tut uns leid, Ihnen mitteilen zu müssen, dass ...
may we remind you that ...	dürfen wir Sie daran erinnern, dass ...
we wish to draw your attention to ...	wir möchten Sie auf ... aufmerksam machen
Requests for payment	
we would appreciate it if you sent us payment promptly	wir würden uns freuen, wenn Sie uns den Rechnungsbetrag bald zukommen ließen
payment is now four weeks overdue	die Zahlung ist jetzt vier Wochen überfällig

an early settlement of your account would be appreciated	eine baldige Begleichung Ihrer Rechnung würden wir begrüßen
we must point out that your bill is still outstanding	wir machen Sie darauf aufmerksam, dass Ihre Rechnung noch aussteht
Ending a letter	
will you please let us have ...	bitte, schicken Sie uns ...
we look forward to receiving ...	wir freuen uns, ... zu erhalten
we trust that you will clear your account in the next few days	wir hoffen, dass Sie Ihre Rechnung in den nächsten Tagen begleichen werden

BRAIN WORK One: Over to you – letter writing

Oh dear, the letter you wrote on the computer is mixed up. There must be a problem with the program! Well, now you must sort out the sentences and put them in the best order.

1. We look forward to hearing from you in the next few days.
2. Dear Mr Free
3. An early settlement of this account would be appreciated.
4. Please find a copy of your invoice attached.
5. Yours sincerely
6. We should like to remind you that payment for order No 439B is a month overdue.
7. If you have already sent a remittance please disregard this letter.

BRAIN WORK Two: What's the English for ...?

Oh no! Your colleague has tried to write another letter but could not remember the English for some words. The result is that there are some German words in these sentences from the letter. Use the information in this chapter to help you put the German words into English.

1. Payment was *fällig* a month ago.
2. Could you please *begleichen* your account as soon as possible?
3. Please *ignorieren* this letter if you have already cleared the account.
4. Thank you for the *Zahlung* of the bill.
5. The *Warenrechnung* has not yet been paid.
6. Please see the *beigeheftete* account.

BRAIN WORK Three: Read and answer the questions

Here and in Brain Work Four are two letters asking for payment. Notice how the character of the language changes in the second letter.
Read the letter and answer the questions.

Dear Sirs 14th August

We are very pleased to let you have enclosed our current brochure and price list. You will note that prices have not increased from last year's and that our products remain the most competitive on the market in terms of both quality and price. You will also be pleased to see that we have extended our range of products.
We look forward to receiving an order from you shortly. We would also like to remind you our account of 1st August has not yet been settled.
You have no doubt overlooked this invoice as you normally settle your account with us promptly.

Yours faithfully

1. What is the writer sending?
2. How does the writer say 'you forgot the bill'?

3. What does the writer want to the reader to note?
4. What does the writer look forward to?
5. Find an alternative word used in the letter for 'pay'.
6. Why does the writer think the bill has not been paid?
7. Is the customer normally good at paying bills?
8. In the letter the writer says that there is something sent together with it. How do you say this in English?

BRAIN WORK Four: How much do you understand?

Read the following letter and answer the questions.

Dear Sirs 21st August

We wish to point out that payment of your bill is now five weeks overdue. We wrote to you on 14th August informing you that your bill had not been settled but we are at a loss to understand why we have had no reply. We must now insist on settlement by 28th August.

Yours faithfully

1. How does the writer say 'we want to make this clear'?
2. 'The payment is five weeks late' but how does the writer say this?
3. How many letters have been written?
4. In the letter how does the writer say 'we find it difficult to understand'?
5. Must payment be on an exact day?

9 Chapter DELAYS IN PAYMENT, PART TWO

Contents

FOCUS: Delays in payment – a final demand
DIALOGUE: Discussing further steps
DROP THEM A LINE: A final demand to Melmoths
PUT IT ANOTHER WAY: Alternative phrases
BRAIN WORK: Complete a letter and do a quiz
LETTER BOX: By and until
More **BRAIN WORK**: Letter box test and new phrases

Joke Time

An employee[1] went to see Bob Onion.
Employee: Excuse me, sir, but I've been working here for over ten years and doing the work of three men. I think it's time I had a rise.
Bob Onion: Well, I must think about giving you a rise but there is no problem about these three men. Give me their names and I'll fire them!

The office boy turned up[2] half an hour late one morning and the boss said, "You should have been here at nine o'clock!"
The office boy looked at the boss and said,"Why, what happened?[3]"

1 Arbeitnehmer, Angestellte 2 auftauchen 3 passieren

FOCUS: Delays in payment – final demands

As we saw in the last chapter, if a customer does not pay on time the seller should write a polite letter enquiring about the delay. If, however, there is no reply or no payment the seller should write again including copies of invoices. Finally, if after the second letter there is still no reply or payment a final demand is sent often giving a last date or deadline. After this time the seller will take some kind of action to get the payment.

DIALOGUE: Discussing further steps

Susan Wright (**SW**) from Sales and the trainee, Terry Jones (**TJ**), are looking at the accounts.

SW: Well, it looks like we need to write to a couple of customers.
TJ: Why? What's wrong?
SW: Some of them just won't pay unless you say things like "We are forced to put the matter in the hands of our solicitor", or "We shall be compelled to take legal proceedings against you."
TJ: What does that mean exactly, pay up or you are in trouble?
SW: In a very simple way, yes. Some people just don't take things seriously unless you threaten them with legal action. That's what I'm going to do with this firm of builders, Melmoths.

Drop them A LINE: Onions' final demand to Melmoths

Onions already phoned and wrote to Melmoths, the builders, but they did not receive an answer or payment so Sue Wright writes the following letter – a final demand:

Dear Mr Melmoth

We have written to you on two occasions, 14th September and 21st November, concerning the outstanding balance for order No 7D34 of £475.75.

We had expected that you would have settled the matter by now but you have offered no explanation for the delay and sent no remittance. Regrettably, unless we receive payment within the next seven days we will be forced to put the matter in the hands of our solicitor.

Yours sincerely
S. Wright

VOCABULARY: To help you understand

account	*Rechnung*
balance	*Kontostand / Saldo begleichen*
concerning	*bezüglich, hinsichtlich*
compel	*zwingen*
couple of	*ein paar*
deadline	*letzter Termin*
delay	*Verzögerung, Verspätung*
enquire	*fragen, erkundigen*
explanation	*Erklärung*
final demand	*letzte Mahnung*
finally	*endlich*
force	*zwingen*
however	*jedoch*
include	*einschließen*
legal proceedings	*Verfahren, Gerichtsverhandlung*
matter	*Sache*
occasion	*Gelegenheit, Anlass*
offer	*anbieten*
outstanding	*ausstehend*
pay up	*zurückzahlen*
polite	*höflich*
rent	*Miete*
rise	*Erhöhung (Geld)*
regrettably	*bedauerlicherweise*
remittance	*Zahlung*
reply	*Antwort*

settle	*erledigen*
solicitor	*Anwalt*
spare parts	*Ersatzteile*
threaten	*drohen*
unless	*es sei denn, wenn nicht*
wrong (what's wrong?)	*was ist los?*

Put it ANOTHER WAY: Alternative phrases

Starting the letter	
we are at a loss to understand why ...	wir können nicht verstehen, warum ...
we note with regret that ...	wir stellen mit Bedauern fest, dass ...
we regret that we ...	wir bedauern, dass wir ...
inspite of two reminders	trotz zweier Mahnungen
we have written to you a number of times	wir haben Ihnen mehrmals geschrieben
Making your point!	
we must insist on payment	wir müssen auf Zahlung bestehen
the account is now three months overdue	die Rechnung ist jetzt drei Monate überfällig
we have no alternative but to ...	uns bleibt nichts anderes übrig, als ...
unless we hear from you within seven days ...	wenn wir innerhalb der nächsten sieben Tage nichts von Ihnen hören ...
we will instruct our solicitors to start proceedings against you	wir werden unsere Rechtsanwälte anweisen, gerichtliche Schritte gegen Sie einzuleiten

if your cheque fails to arrive within ...	falls Ihr Scheck nicht innerhalb ... eintrifft
Ending the letter	
please pay the account and settle this matter without further delay	begleichen Sie bitte die Rechnung ohne weitere Verzögerung
we hope that you will deal with this matter as soon as possible	wir hoffen, dass Sie diese Angelegenheit so bald wie möglich erledigen

BRAIN WORK One: Complete the letter

Here is a chance to see what you can remember. Below are some words and phrases. Use each one once to complete the sentences.

regrettably insist outstanding solicitor remittance reminders

1. In spite of two ... you have still not settled your account.
2. We must ... on payment within seven days.
3. We will put the matter in the hands of our ....
4. ..., if your cheque fails to arrive tomorrow, we will be forced to instruct our solicitors to start proceedings against you.
5. Your account has been ... for three months.
6. We look forward to receiving your ... next week.

BRAIN WORK Two: What's the English for ...?

Here are some English words with letters missing. Please add the letters to complete the word. The German for the words is below to help you but not in the correct order!

bezüglich Zahlung es sei denn ausstehend Verzögerung

1. r-mitt-nc-	2. -onc-rni-g	3. d-l-y	4. o-tst-ndi-ng	5. u-le-s

BRAIN WORK Three: Quiz time

Have a try at this little quiz. Good luck! Circle one letter for the correct answer.

1. A "remittance" is an alternative word for **a** delay **b** payment **c** letter	**2.** A third letter asking for payment is also called **a** an invoice **b** a final demand **c** a last request
3. An "outstanding account" is **a** a very positive bank balance **b** a bill that is not paid **c** a cheque sent by post	**4.** If you "attach" a copy to a letter you **a** send the copy separately **b** fix the copy to the letter **c** fax the copy with the letter

LETTER BOX: By and until

Most people have problems with "by" and "until". This is because in German both words can be translated by "bis". Look at the two sentences below to see the diference.

1) *I will be in Paris until Tuesday.*
2) *I will be in Paris by Tuesday (at the latest).*

Sentence 1) means that I am in Paris at the moment and I will leave on Tuesday.

Sentence 2) means I am not in Paris at the moment but I will be in Paris on Saturday, Sunday or anytime before or on Tuesday. I will be in Paris on Tuesday at the latest.

Note the sentences:

1) *We will make payment until 1st January.*
2) *We will make payment by 1st January (at the latest).*

Sentence 1) means several payments are made, the last one on 1st January.

Sentence 2) means one payment made between now and 1st January.

To help you remember the difference note that the "mindestens haltbar" sign on food is called "use / sell by date" in English. You can only use a litre of milk one time before the date. You cannot drink the milk again and again! As another tip, ask yourself is the action one time (by) or several, continual actions (until)?

Brain Work Four: A little work on "by" and "until"

Okay, let's see if you can see the difference between by and until. In the sentences put in until or by. Remember that you can say at the latest (*spätestens*) with by.

1. I will arrive at the airport ... 7o'clock. My flight is at 9.25.
2. I will be on the train ... 10.40. I arrive in London at 10.40.
3. We will supply spare parts ... you sell the machine.
4. The rent must be paid ... the first of the month.
5. Please pay the remittance ... the end of the week.

BRAIN WORK Five: Please correct the errors

The following letter contains errors. Find and correct the ten mistakes. You should read this chapter again carefully before you do this exercise.

Dear Ms Crook

This is the third occasions that we have writing to you to concerning the outstanding balance for £4,789 for order No 6719.
We had expect that you would have paid the bill until now but you have sent us no remittance or offered us no explanation four the delay.
Regrettably, until you made the payment within the next seven day we will be force to put the matter in the hands of our legal department.

Yours sincerely
Edward Nicely

BRAIN WORK Six: Using new vocabulary

Here are a number of sentences. Please change them using the alternative words or phrases.

1. We do not understand why the payment has not been made.
2. If the cheque does not arrive within seven days we will contact our solicitor.
3. Please explain why you have sent no payment.
4. We have written to you two times concerning the outstanding balance.
5. Unless we get the remittance we will put the matter in the hands of our legal team.
6. We are unhappy concerning the bill, which has not been paid.

a receive
b we are at a loss to
c fails to arrive
d remittance
e on two occasions
f the outstanding account

10 Chapter

APOLOGIES

Contents

Joke Time

In Onions the boss of the sales department asked the new junior[1]:
"Have you posted those two things I gave you, you know, the letter to Sydney and that little parcel of components[2] to Manchester?"
"I have," said the junior full of pride[3], "and what's more, I put right that mistake you made with the postage."
"How do you mean?" said the boss surprised.
"Well, you put £8.20 worth of stamps on the local parcel and only a stamp for 80p on that letter to Australia. Don't worry, I sorted it out[4]. I just changed the addresses."

1 Büroaushilfe 2 Komponenten 3 Stolz 4 erledigen

FOCUS: Apologies – saying sorry

It sometimes happens that in business you will need to say sorry and explain a difficult situation. If there is a delay in payment, for example, you should write to the supplier and give reasons for the hold up. Perhaps you can make alternative suggestions about payment or the supply of a product. This is simple courtesy.
Do not forget that the people you are doing business with have debts and deadlines too. Also, do not forget that it is good business practice.
Maybe you will need to do business with this firm again. Even if you do not, you will do business with another firm and 'word gets around'. It is not good for your business if people think you are unreliable.

DIALOGUE: John Melmoth finds out what went wrong

The boss of Melmoths, John Melmoth (**JM**), comes back to the office after being away for three months. He left his son, Kevin (**KM**), in charge.

JM: A final demand from Onions? Good grief! Why didn't you pay the bill before?

KM: We've had a few problems keeping up with the correspondence side. Sandra left two months ago and we had trouble finding another secretary, so, you know Marvin's sister, nice girl, well, she had a go at the job.

JM: Had a go! You mean Marvin who works for us? His sister? Well, if she's as smart as he is I expect that letters were badly typed, replies lost, faxes sent to wrong place ...

KM: Well, don't worry, she didn't do that, in fact she didn't do anything. She left after two days.

JM: And then what?

KM: We hired a girl from the agency. She seemed very good until we found out how she dealt with the correspondence. One evening I moved a filing cabinet from the office and found all these letters behind it.

JM: So you fired her!
KM: That's right. We got another secretary, from a different agency, but she left ...
JM: After a week?
KM: After one morning, trying to sort out the mess the other girl made.
JM: Well, it looks like I've got some letter writing, phoning and thinking up excuses to do!

Drop them A LINE: Melmoths say sorry to Onions

John Melmoth thought about what he would say. After a while he puts pen to paper and writes a letter to Onions explaining why they have not received a bill:

Dear Mrs Wright

We were indeed very sorry to receive your final demand for our order No 7D34 for the amount of £475.75.
The cause of the considerable delay was due entirely to circumstances beyond our control.
I enclose a cheque for the amount and very much regret the inconvenience this delay has caused you. I also hope that this delay will not have a negative effect on our future business relationship and assure you that delays will not occur in future.

Yours sincerely
J. Melmoth.

VOCABULARY: To help you understand

agency	*Agentur*
amount	*Betrag*
assure; ~ somebody of something	*jemandem etwas versichern*
beyond our control	*nicht in unserer Hand liegend*

business practice	*Geschäftspraxis*
business relationship	*Geschäftsbeziehung*
cause	*verursachen / Ursache*
charge; be in ~	*verantwortlich sein, die Verantwortung haben*
circumstance	*Umstand*
considerable	*groß, erheblich*
courtesy	*Höflichkeit*
debts	*Schulden*
due to	*infolge*
entirely	*völlig*
excuse	*Ausrede*
explain	*erklären*
filing cabinet	*Aktenschrank*
future	*Zukunft*
good grief!	*Mein Gott!*
have a go at something	*versuchen, etwas zu tun*
have trouble	*Probleme haben*
hire	*einstellen*
hold up	*Verzögerung, Verspätung*
inconvenience	*Unannehmlichkeit*
junior	*Bürogehilfe*
keep up with	*Schritt halten mit*
occur	*vorkommen*
postage	*Porto*
pride	*Stolz*
reply / replies	*Antwort / en*
sales department	*Verkaufsabteilung*
sort out	*erledigen*
suggestion	*Vorschlag*
supplier	*Lieferant*
surprised	*überrascht*
think up	*erfinden, ausdenken*
unreliable	*unzuverlässig*
word gets round that ...	*man munkelt, dass ...*

Put It ANOTHER WAY: Alternative phrases

Starting a letter	
we very much regret	wir bedauern sehr
please accept our apologies for	wir bitten um Entschuldigung wegen
we are extremely sorry	es tut uns äußerst leid
Reasons for delay	
business has been slack	das Geschäft geht schlecht
we are in difficulties as our main customer has gone bankrupt	wir sind in Schwierigkeiten gekommen, weil unser Hauptkunde Konkurs gemacht hat
our customers have recently been slow in meeting their obligations	unsere Kunden kommen in der letzten Zeit ihren Verpflichtungen schleppend nach
our present problems are only temporary	unsere gegenwärtigen Schwierigkeiten sind nur vorübergehend
we are experiencing great difficulty in collecting payment	wir haben erhebliche Schwierigkeiten beim Einzug unserer Rechnungen
Promising payment	
you will find enclosed a cheque for ... in full settlement of your bill	wir fügen einen Scheck über ... zum vollen Ausgleich Ihrer Rechnung bei
we will clear the outstanding amount by the end of this month	wir werden die ausstehende Summe bis Ende dieses Monats begleichen
please be good enough to grant us a few weeks in which to pay	bitte seien Sie so freundlich und gewähren Sie uns noch einige Wochen zur Zahlung

we are making every effort to pay the bill by the end of November	wir werden alle Anstrengungen unternehmen, um die Rechnung bis Ende November zu bezahlen
we have today instructed our bank to transfer ... to your account	heute haben wir unsere Bank angewiesen ... auf Ihr Konto zu überweisen

BRAIN WORK One: What's the English for ...?

Now you can put the English word together with the German word.

1. inconvenience	**a** Antwort
2. occur	**b** Verzögerung
3. hold up	**c** Unannehmlichkeit
4. assure	**d** vorkommen
5. considerable	**e** versichern
6. reply	**f** groß, erheblich

BRAIN WORK Two: Complete the sentences

Time for you to see what you remember. Use the words below to complete the sentences. Use each word only once.

assure enclose inconvenience beyond receive

1. We were very sorry to ... your final demand.
2. The cause of the delay was ... our control.
3. We ... a cheque for the amount.
4. We also regret the ... this delay has caused you.
5. I wish to ... you that this delay in payment will not occur again.

BRAIN WORK Three: A little translating

Here is a letter explaining the reason for a delay and asking for more time to pay. The letter is in English but some of the words are in German. Please put the words in English. Use the phrases from this chapter to help you.

Dear Sir

Wir bedauern sehr the delay in payment of your *Rechnung* No B527 for £102.50. The reason for the *Verzögerung* is that *wir in Schwierigkeiten gekommen sind* because our *Kunden kommen in der letzten Zeit ihren Verpflichtungen schleppend nach.*
We *versichern* you that our *gegenwärtige Schwierigkeiten* are only *vorübergehend* and we will clear the *ausstehende* amount *bis Ende dieses Monats.*

Yours faithfully

BRAIN WORK Four: Improve your powers to see mistakes!

Here are six sentences but each one contains one error. Find and correct these errors.

We regret very much the delay in delevery.
We is in difficulties as our main customer has gone bankrupt.
The reason for the delay were beyond our control.
We are made every effort to pay the bill by Tuesday of next week.
Please find a cheque of £200 enclosed.
We are happy to grant you two more week in which to deliver.

DELAYS IN DELIVERY

Chapter 11

DELAYS IN DELIVERY

Contents

FOCUS: Delays in delivery – breaking a contract
DIALOGUE: Singapore is late with a delivery to Onions
DROP THEM A LINE: Onions complain about the delay and a fax from Mr Wung
PUT IT ANOTHER WAY: Alternative phrases
BRAIN WORK: A quiz and sort out a letter

Joke Time

Back at Onions, in Bob Onion's Office:
Secretary: Excuse me, Mr Onion, but I think that somebody wants to talk to you on the phone.
Bob Onion: Now, what on earth does that mean, young woman? Listen, does somebody want to speak to me or not? You think that somebody wants to talk to me?
Secretary: Well, Mr Onion, all I can say is that the caller asked if the 'senile old fool' was in the office, so I wasn't sure if you wanted to take it.

FOCUS: Delays in delivery – breaking a contract

Clearly, if a supplier is late delivering goods or does not deliver the goods at all he/she has broken a contract. This is called a breach of contract. Here is an example letter for the worst case:

Dear Sirs

The long delays in the execution of your orders is of great concern to us. Over the past months we have contacted you concerning delays and you have made various promises to us. In good faith we have informed our customers that goods would arrive in good time. In virtually every case you have let us down and as a consequence our customers no longer believe us.
As a result of this failure to deliver on time or at all, a number of our best customers are cancelling orders. We estimate that we have already lost £40,000 of cancelled orders due to your inability to deliver as agreed. This is an extremely unsatisfactory situation as it has led to a loss, not only of business, but also confidence in ourselves. You may be assured this will have serious results for our company and yours.

Yours faithfully

DIALOGUE: Singapore is late with a delivery to Onions

At the purchasing department in Onions the production manager, Nick James (**NJ**), is discussing a delay in the delivery with one of the buyers, Sue Weakly (**SW**).

NJ: What's the problem with the electric motors we ordered from that firm in Singapore? We only have about twenty left in stock and we will need fifty for that new order.

SW: Well, we have not done much business with them before. We used to get 70% of our motors from Britain and the rest from Germany.

NJ: Yes, and who decided to place an order with a firm in Singapore?

SW: Actually, I decided to do it because the British firms could not produce enough and on time and the German firm was too expensive. Anyway I have already written to them. Here's the letter.

NJ: Yes, but at least the German firm was reliable. Well, hopefully we'll get a reply or the motors next week. You know that all this sending letters is very fine but we need the motors.

Drop Them A LINE: Onions complain about the delay

Sue Weakly wrote to the Singapore company and here is the letter:

Dear Mr Wung

On 14th June we placed an order for 120 electric motors type M200 produced by you (order No A564).
You assured us that you could supply the motors from stock and we would receive them within eight weeks. Nine weeks have now passed and we are still not in receipt of the consignment.
As we pointed out when we ordered, a prompt delivery was essential. Since we require the motors urgently we regret that we shall be compelled to cancel the order if the shipment does not arrive by the end of the month.

Yours sincerely
S. Weakly

Shortly after Onions received a fax:

Fax to: S Weakly, Purchasing; Onion Engineering 0044 121/345655
Fax from: T Wung Date 07.08.20..

Dear Sir

Very sorry about overdue shipment of motors. We are pleased to report the goods were shipped on the SS Voyager on 20th June. Our shipping agent informs us that due to bad weather the ship was delayed for a week. He assures us that you will receive your goods within the week.

Yours sincerely
T Wung

VOCABULARY: To help you understand

agreed	*vereinbart*
anyway	*trotzdem, jedenfalls*
assume	*annehmen*
at all	*überhaupt*
at least	*mindestens*
believe	*glauben*
breach of contract	*Vertragsbruch*
caller	*Anrufer*
cancel	*stornieren*
clearly	*offensichtlich*
compel	*zwingen*
concern	*Sorge, Besorgnis*
concerning	*bezüglich*
confidence	*Vertrauen*
consequence	*Folge*
consignment	*Sendung*
contract	*Vertrag*
do business	*Geschäfte machen*
due to	*wegen*
essential	*sehr wichtig*
estimate	*schätzen*
execution	*Ausführung*
expensive	*teuer*
extremely	*äußerst*
failure	*Mißerfolg, Scheitern*
faith; in good ~	*in gutem Glauben*
from stock	*ab Lager*
good time; in ~	*rechtzeitig*
hopefully	*hoffentlich*
inability	*Unfähigkeit*
lead to	*dazu führen*
let down	*enttäuschen*
loss	*Verlust*
lost	*verloren*
overdue	*überfällig*

pass	*vergehen*
past	*vergangen*
point out	*betonen*
promise	*Versprechen*
receipt; in ~	*im Besitz*
reliable	*zuverlässig*
ship	*versenden*
shipment	*Sendung*
shipping agent	*Reedereivertreter*
stock; in ~	*auf Lager*
unsatisfactory	*nicht zufriedenstellend*
urgently	*dringend*
various	*verschieden*
virtually	*nahezu*
what on earth!	*Was in aller Welt!*

Put it ANOTHER WAY: Alternative phrases

Starting	
the goods ordered by us on 12th June	die von uns am 12. Juni bestellten Waren
our letter of 21st November has not been answered	unser Brief vom 21. November ist nicht beantwortet worden
we are sorry to inform you that ...	es tut uns leid, Ihnen mitteilen zu müssen, dass ...
we are forced to complain about the delay in delivery	wir müssen uns über den Lieferverzug beschweren
Complaining	
the delay puts us in a difficult position	der Verzug bringt uns in eine schwierige Lage
an early delivery was guaranteed	eine prompte Lieferung wurde garantiert

complying with the delivery dates is essential	die Einhaltung der Liefertermine ist äußerst wichtig
the delay was more than three weeks	der Verzug betrug mehr als drei Wochen
we must insist that you observe delivery dates for future orders	wir müssen darauf bestehen, dass Sie bei künftigen Bestellungen die Liefertermine beachten
Ending	
we will be pleased to have your explanation for the long delay	wir wären für eine Erklärung der langen Verzögerung dankbar
we ask you to look into the matter	wir bitten Sie, die Angelegenheit zu untersuchen
please hasten the delivery	bitte bringen Sie die Lieferung schnell auf den Weg

BRAIN WORK One: A little quiz

Now try and put in the correct word into each sentence. There are three possible words but only one correct word.

1. The firm ... us that the goods would arrive on time.
   a compelled   b assured   c overdue
2. The long ... in the execution of your order is unsatisfactory.
   a consignment   b reliable   c delay
3. If the goods do not arrive next week we will ... the order.
   a cancel   b sign   c lengthen
4. We ... the order last month.
   a contracted   b stocked   c placed
5. Three weeks have ... but we still do not have the shipment.
   a executed   b passed   c replied

BRAIN WORK Two: Sort out the letter

Here are parts of a letter complaining about a delay in delivery. Please put them in the best order.

1. That was three weeks ago.
2. We are forced to complain about the delay in our order No D546.
3. We will be compelled to cancel the consignment if the goods do not arrive by next week.
4. You assured us that the goods would be here within a week.
5. The delay puts us in a difficult position as we need the goods urgently.
6. We will be pleased to receive your explanation.

BRAIN WORK Three: Test your vocabulary

Here are some key words from the last chapter. They have been mixed up. What are they?

1. veroued
2. cexeiontu
3. hips
4. yurglent
5. fidnecenoc
6. tailneess

Ausführung   sehr wichtig   überfällig   dringend   Vertrauen   versenden

12 Chapter ARRANGING A MEETING

ARRANGING A MEETING

Contents

FOCUS: Arranging meetings to develop personal relations
DIALOGUE: Talking about style in making arrangements
DROP THEM A LINE: Arranging a meeting
PUT IT ANOTHER WAY: Alternative phrases
BRAIN WORK: What's the English for ...? and a translation
LETTER BOX: Prepositions of time
More **BRAIN WORK**: Letter box test

Joke Time

"No way![1]" said the boss. "I cannot give you two hours off for lunch. Think man, if I did that I would have to do the same for every person whose wife had just had triplets[2]."

1 Kommt nicht in Frage! 2 Drillinge

FOCUS: Arranging meetings to develop personal relations

It is very important to make and develop personal relations in business. Although the telephone is useful in communicating, very often a meeting can quickly clear up problems and establish good business contacts. Meetings can be arranged by phone but as always in business, it is always good practice to finalize details in writing. Look at the short letter below:

Dear Mrs Lewis

I would appreciate it very much if I could have the opportunity of meeting you personally so that we can discuss future business. As I hope to be in London from 12th to 15th June I thought that it would be possible to meet then. I shall contact your office by phone on my arrival.
Please let me know if you will be free to see me and what time would be best for you.

Regards
Jack Beam

DIALOGUE: Talking about style in making arrangements

In the purchasing department Jane Parker (**JP**) is talking to a trainee, Rose Hill (**RH**).

JP: Well, on the phone you can say things like 'Can we meet up on Wednesday?' or 'If it's okay with you, how about Wednesday?'. But when you confirm an arrangement in writing then you need to be a little more formal.

RH: Alright, let's say I phone up and say that I will be in the area and I want to see somebody in sales, to discuss an order. I'll be staying at a hotel. If it's alright with you we can fix up a time on such and such a date. Oh yeah, and let us know if you can make it then, before I leave.

JP: We need to think about this. Let's write a letter and say what you want but in good style.

RH: Of course, there is another thing about letters.

JP: And what is that? You mean it's always good to get things on paper to avoid confusion later, like on the phone?

RH: No, it means that every time I arrange a room for a visitor at the King George Hotel I don't have the macho manager chatting me up!

Drop Them A LINE: Arranging a meeting

That's how Rose's letter looks:

Dear Mrs Smith

As I will be in Manchester on Monday and Tuesday of next week I would be very pleased if I could arrange to meet you with a view to discussing a new order.
I will be staying in the Royal Hotel near the city centre. Could you please leave a message at reception informing me when it would be convenient to meet.
I would be grateful if you could get in touch with me prior to my departure to say if you will be in the firm during this time. If we can meet I will bring the information and catalogue detailing the equipment you were interested in.
Hoping that we will be able to meet. I look forward to seeing you then.

Yours sincerely
Miss Hill, purchasing

VOCABULARY: To help you understand

although	*obwohl*
avoid	*vermeiden*
chat me up	*mich anquatschen*
convenient time	*passende Zeit*
departure	*Abreise*
develop	*entwickeln*

establish	*gründen, bilden*
finalize	*endgültig festlegen*
fix up	*arrangieren*
get in touch with	*sich in Verbindung setzen*
grateful	*dankbar*
make it (can you make it?)	*es schaffen (schaffen Sie es?)*
meet up	*treffen*
message	*Nachricht*
on my arrival	*bei meiner Ankunft*
opportunity	*Möglichkeit*
practice	*Gewohnheit, Verfahrensweise*
prior to	*vor, bevor*
reception	*Empfang*
relation	*Beziehung*
useful	*nützlich*
with a view to	*mit der Absicht, etwas zu tun*

Put it ANOTHER WAY: Alternative phrases

To start	
I would welcome the opportunity to ...	ich würde die Gelegenheit begrüßen, um ...
I would like to call on you	ich würde Sie gern aufsuchen..
Fixing date and time	
would 2 o'clock on Friday be convenient?	würde Ihnen Freitag um 14.00 Uhr passen?
I would be pleased / happy / glad if you would suggest a time and date to ...	ich würde mich freuen, wenn Sie eine Zeit und Datum vorschlagen würden, um ...
... please give me a ring. a message will reach me in the office	bitte rufen Sie mich an. Eine Nachricht wird mich im Büro erreichen

if this time/day does not suit you	falls diese Zeit/dieser Tag Ihnen nicht passt
please suggest an alternative day	bitte schlagen Sie einen anderen Tag vor
would it be at all possible to arrange another meeting?	wäre es überhaupt möglich, einen anderen Termin zu vereinbaren?
Ending the letter	
I look forward to meeting you	ich freue mich, Sie zu treffen
it will be a pleasure to see you again	ich freue mich darauf, Sie wiederzusehen
I will be delighted to meet you	ich freue mich sehr, Sie zu treffen

BRAIN WORK One: What's the English for ...?

Over to you! Please put the English word together with the German word.

1. convenient	obwohl
2. grateful	Ankunft
3. opportunity	passend
4. although	dankbar
5. arrival	vor/bevor
6. prior to	Möglichkeit

BRAIN WORK Two: Letter writing

Now your turn to do a little work on a letter. Here is a letter partly in German. Please use the phrases and vocabulary in this chapter to replace the German with English.

Dear Mr Barker

Ich würde die Gelegenheit begrüßen to meet you some time next week. *Würde Ihnen Dienstag um 10.00 passen? Falls* this day and time are not convenient *bitte schlagen Sie eine andere Zeit und einen anderen Tag vor.*
Please contact me in the company. If I am out *eine Nachricht wird mich im Büro erreichen.*
Ich freue mich sehr, Sie wieder zu treffen

Yours sincerely
A. Lowe, Sales

LETTER BOX: Prepositions of time

Prepositions of time can be a little tricky but if you look at the examples below you should not make a mistake.

at 9 o'clock / 6.30 a.m.
at midday / midnight
at Easter / Christmas
at the end of March / the moment
at the weekend(s)

on Friday(s) / Monday(s) etc.
on 12th August / 30th April etc.
on Christmasday / Good Friday (Karfreitag)

in June / December
in 1958 / 1066 / 2005
in (the) spring / autumn / summer / winter
in the afternoon / the evening / the morning

Note: on Monday afternoon / on Friday morning

BRAIN WORK Three: Prepositions of time

Please put in the correct preposition of time in the sentences below. Use the information in the Letter Box to help you. Good luck!

1. We will make the delivery ... August.
2. I sent you a fax ... Tuesday afternoon last week.
3. We shall meet you at the airport ... 12 o'clock.
4. The company was established ... 1885 by my great great grandfather.
5. The sales manager will visit your firm some time ... late summer.
6. Our firm does not work ... Wednesday afternoon.
7. We do not work ... the weekends.

BRAIN WORK Four: A little puzzle with vocabulary

Here are six typical sentences from this chapter. The problem is that they have been mixed up. What should each sentence really say?

1. Seeing I look to forward you.
2. We call would like to on you.
3. Suggest date please an alternative.
4. Please ring me a give as soon as arrive you.
5. I would welcome you the opportunity of meeting.
6. It would arrange be possible to meeting another next month.

MORE ON MEETINGS

Chapter 13

MORE ON MEETINGS

Contents

FOCUS: Answering invitations to a meeting
DIALOGUE: Bob Onion expects a visit from Russia
DROP THEM A LINE: The reply to the Russians
PUT IT ANOTHER WAY: Alternative phrases
BRAIN WORK: What's the English for ...? plus a little more

Joke Time

Bob Onion called in one of his salesmen[1].
"Sidebottom, you dress well[2], even smartly[3], you are charming in the office and very friendly."
"Well, thank you, sir. I do my best for the firm," said Sidebottom slightly surprised[4] and now expecting a raise.
"That's okay. I was just trying to put you in a good mood[5] before we start to discuss the fact that you are often late, have days off work when you feel like it and have the lowest sales performance[6] in the office."

1 Verkäufer 2 gut angezogen 3 schick 4 etwas überrascht 5 gute Laune 6 niedrigster Umsatz

FOCUS: Answering invitations to a meeting

If invited to meet a customer either by letter or phone a written response in the form of a letter is very important. This can avoid misunderstandings that at times happen when arrangements are made only on the phone. It is also an opportunity to build up business relationships and good will. Take a look at the letter below.

Dear Mr Nixon

Thank you for your letter dated 21st June of this year informing us that your chief overseas buyer, Mrs McCartney, will be coming to Europe in August. I shall be delighted to meet her then with a view to discussing a number of projects. Please contact me nearer her planned date of arrival. If Mrs McCartney wishes we will be happy to meet her at the airport and arrange accommodation for the duration of her stay.
I very much look forward to meeting Mrs McCartney

Yours sincerely
L. Bronstein

DIALOGUE: Bob Onion expects a visit from Russia

Bob Onion (**BO**) is talking to his new sales manager, Fiona Merryweather (**FM**). He has just received a letter from the Russian engineering company, Popov Engineering International.

BO: You must listen to this letter! (*Bob Onion reads the letter*)

Dear Mr Onion
A group of our representatives will be in England next month.
We would be glad to visit you in your company with a view to developing business relations. Mr Podgorny, who visited you last year, will also be there. We will be in Birmingham on 14th to the 17th August and we hope that you will be able to meet our representatives then. Please contact us with your comments. We look forward to hearing from you shortly.

Yours sincerely
A. Popov

FM: Isn't that nice, keeping contact and so on?
BO: This is dreadful news. This Podgorny chap was here last year.
FM: Yes, but didn't you make a deal worth £15,000?
BO: Absolutely right.They are acting as our agents now. We also had to put him in a hotel for weekend then pay the bill.
FM: Well, that's nothing in comparison.
BO: Oh no? There were one or two extras.
FM: That's normal too!
BO: While he was here I had to accompany him virtually everywhere he went. I had a hangover for five days and this time a group of them are coming! No, write and tell them I'm on holiday, in hospital, in prison or gone to become a monk in a monastry. You and your colleagues can deal with it. That's what you are paid for.
FM: Mmm! Mr Abdul Azis from Saudi will be here, too. Maybe Mr Podgorny could show him round.
BO: I do hope that you are pulling my leg. I don't think they will have a lot in common apart from buying our products, I hope. Oh, and another thing, last year it was just Popov Ltd.
FM: Well?
BO: Now they are Popov International. Lord help us!

Drop Them A LINE: The reply to the Russians

Following the conversation between Onion and Merryweather, Popov gets a letter from Onions:

Dear Mr Popov

It is with considerable regret that I have to advise you that Mr Onion will be away for the first two weeks of August. However, myself and other members of the sales department will be pleased to welcome you.
Please get in touch with us as soon as you arrive in England.
Yours sincerely

Fiona Merryweather
Sales Manager

VOCABULARY: To help you understand

able to do; be ~	*etwas können, fähig sein*
accommodation	*Unterkunft*
accompany	*begleiten*
advise	*informieren/mitteilen*
arrival	*Ankunft*
avoid	*vermeiden*
chap	*Kerl*
charming	*charmant*
chief	*Haupt-*
common	*gemeinsam*
comparison	*Vergleich*
considerable; with ~ regret	*mit großem Bedauern*
day off	*Tag frei*
delighted	*entzückt*
dreadful	*schrecklich*
duration	*Dauer*
glad	*froh*
good mood	*gute Laune*
good will	*Wohlwollen*
hangover	*Kater*
invite	*einladen*
invitation	*Einladung*
member	*Mitglied*
monk	*Mönch*
opportunity	*Möglichkeit*
overseas	*Übersee*
performance	*Leistung*
pull somebody's leg	*jemanden auf den Arm nehmen*
regret	*Bedauern*
representative	*Vertreter*
response	*Antwort*
right	*richtig*
shortly	*bald*

slightly	*etwas, ein kleines bisschen*
smart	*schick*
stay	*Aufenthalt*
virtually	*fast*
with a view to	*mit der Absicht, etwas zu tun*

Put It ANOTHER WAY: Alternative phrases

unfortunately the manager is in Japan at the moment	leider ist der Manager zurzeit in Japan
I am afraid that I must cancel the meeting with the export manager	leider muss ich die Besprechung mit dem Exportleiter absagen
I am sorry that I had call you to postpone the meeting	es tut mir Leid, dass ich Sie anrufen musste, um die Zusammenkunft zu verschieben
I expect to be back in the office on Tuesday	ich nehme an, dass ich am Dienstag wieder im Büro sein werde
would it be convenient for you to meet me for lunch?	wäre es Ihnen recht, wenn wir uns zum Mittagessen treffen?
thank you for your kind invitation	danke für Ihre freundliche Einladung
it is most kind of you to invite me to dinner on Wednesday	es ist äußerst freundlich von Ihnen, mich am Mittwoch zum Mittagessen einzuladen
it will be good to see you again	ich freue mich, Sie wiederzusehen
I cannot accept your invitation owing to a previous engagement	ich kann Ihre Einladung wegen einer früheren Verpflichtung nicht annehmen

BRAIN WORK One: What's the English for ...?

To test your memory put the English and German words together.

1.	postpone	**a**	bedauern
2.	convenient	**b**	verschieben
3.	cancel	**c**	Einladung
4.	at the moment	**d**	passend
5.	regret	**e**	absagen
6.	invitation	**f**	augenblicklich

BRAIN WORK Two: Complete the sentences

Please put in the words below into the sentences and check the meaning with the words in this chapter.

expect kind owing afraid unfortunately convenient

1. ... I cannot meet you for dinner tomorrow.
2. Would it be ... to meet you in two weeks?
3. I want to thank you for your ... invitation.
4. ... to a previous engagement I cannot see you next Monday.
5. I am ... that I must postpone the meeting.
6. I ... to be in London on 19th May.

BRAIN WORK Three: Let's look at a few words

Here are some words from this chapter with letters missing. Please complete the word and give the German for it.

1. in-i-ati-n	means	....	in German
2. -pp-rt-n-ty		....	
3. r-sp-n-e		....	
4. ov-rs—s		....	
5. -cco-mod-t-on		....	
6. p-rform-n-e		....	

BRAIN WORK Four: A little translation work

Here is a letter about arranging a meeting. It contains a number of German words. Translate them please to make a perfect letter using the English words following the letter.

Ich würde es sehr begrüßen if I could have the *Gelegenheit* of meeting you on my *bevorstehenden Besuch* to Palma. I will be in Palma from Monday 9th April until Thursday 12th where I will be staying at the hotel 'Azul Verano'. *Ich werde mich mit Ihrem Büro bei meiner Ankunft telefonisch in Verbindung setzen*. I would be grateful if you could *mir mitteilen* the day and time which would *passen* you but I would prefer the afternoon of Wednesday 10th.
If the day and time suggested *Ihnen nicht passen* please let me know and suggest another date for a meeting.
I look forward *auf das Vergnügen* of seeing you and your production team then.

suit
to the pleasure
I shall contact your office by telephone on my arrival
chance
are inconvenient
I should very much appreciate it
forthcoming visit
let me know

14 Chapter COMPLAINTS

Contents

FOCUS: Complaining customer
DIALOGUE: Onions receive the wrong order
DROP THEM A LINE: Onions complain and get a reply. Other complaints.
PUT IT ANOTHER WAY: Alternative phrases
BRAIN WORK: Complete a letter and solve a quiz

Joke Time

The boss: Good grief, this letter is full of mistakes. The punctuation[1] is dreadful[2] and the spelling is lousy[3]! Didn't you check it to see if it was okay?
The secretary: I would have but didn't you say that the letter was strictly private and confidential[4]?

1 Zeichensetzung 2 schrecklich 3 lausig 4 streng vertraulich

FOCUS: Complaining customer

A customer may complain about a number of different things. The goods may be defective or spoilt in some way. They may have been damaged during transport.
The goods received by the customer may not correspond to type, quality or quantity ordered. If the seller fails to deliver as agreed the goods will be placed at his / her disposal. Any payment made by the buyer should be refunded. If the buyer still wants to have the goods he / she does not annul the contract but rather asks for replacements. To promote goodwill the seller should always be ready to admit an error. Often, seller and buyer will reach compromises. Only in the worst cases do firms settle difficulties by going to law. This costs a lot of money and wastes time.

DIALOGUE: Onions receive the wrong order

One Monday, Robin Hodgeson (**RH**), manager of the store of Onions, comes into the purchasing department to talk to Ian Miller (**IM**), one of the buyers.

RH: We had a delivery last week of copper pipes from Tyzacks and I think you should know that there are a few problems.

IM: Really? What problems?

RH: When we opened the crate we saw they had sent 150 T-joints instead of 300 bends. They also sent us 400 plastic brackets.

IM: We didn't order any brackets, plastic or metal.

RH: What do you want me to do with them?

IM: I'll drop them a line and ask them what's going on.

RH: Okay, but in the meantime we need the bends. What do you think?

IM: Bends? I'll just have to see what Tyzacks say. Maybe they can send us the bends straight away by special delivery.

IM: Well, sorry about the joke but the engineers are complaining about not having bends and it's driving me right round the bend!

IM: Very funny, but I've heard that joke before in this company.

Drop Them A LINE: Onions complain and get a reply

Here is the letter Ian wrote to Tyzacks:

For the attention of the Sales Department

Dear Sirs

I regret that I must call your attention to the last order you sent us, order no P460, which arrived on 13th June. Although most of the order was correct, you have sent us a box of 150 T-joints marked F104 instead of the 300 bends we actually ordered. In addition the crate contained 400 plastic brackets which we did not order.
Although we may need the T-joints in the future we have no requirement for brackets. As well as this we need the 300 bends urgently.
Please let us have your comments with regard to this matter.

Yours faithfully
Ian Miller

With good business practice, a company should always reply to a complaint. Here is the reply from Tyzacks to Onions:

Dear Mr Miller

Thank you for your letter dated 16th June concerning order no P460.
I am both surprised and sorry to hear about the problems with the make up of the order. I am sure you will agree that we are a regular and reliable supplier and this is the first time that such an error has occurred. I will despatch a box of 300 bends to you immediately by special delivery. As far as the brackets are concerned I shall arrange to pick them up next week. Please inform me if you wish to keep the T-joints. I am willing to grant a 10% discount on this item for causing you inconvenience.

Yours sincerely
Barry Noble

Here are some other complaints

Citroflip, a tropical fruit distributor and wholesaler, writes to a supplier:

Dear Sirs

We were most disappointed with the latest delivery of mixed fruit.
The bananas were overripe and could not be sold and half the oranges had clearly been badly bruised while being shipped.
In addition, we found, upon weighing the dried dates that every bag was two or three pounds underweight.
We trust you will look into this matter and let us know as soon as possible what action you intend to take.

Yours faithfully

A department store writes to a clothing supplier:

Dear Sirs

We are sorry to report that upon careful inspection of your recent consignment of woollen socks we found that the quality did not correspond to that of the samples you originally sent us.
When placing the order we stressed the importance of high quality as our customers are accustomed to only the best.
We can only assume that this is an oversight on your part. If not, and you are unable to supply us, we will be forced to terminate the contract and take our custom elsewhere.
We must ask you to take prompt action as we cannot sell these socks and there is great demand for such items due to the present cold weather.
We await your reply with interest.

Yours faithfully

VOCABULARY: To help you understand

accustomed to	*gewöhnt daran*
actually	*eigentlich, in der Tat*
addition; in ~	*außerdem*

admit	*zugeben*
agreed; as ~	*vereinbaren (wie vereinbart)*
annul	*annullieren*
as far as ... is concerned	*was ... betrifft*
assure	*versichern*
attention; for the ~ of ...	*zu Händen von ....*
badly bruised (fruit)	*(Obst) mit schlimmen Druckstellen*
bend	*Bogen*
box	*Karton*
bracket	*Anschluss*
case	*Fall*
cause	*verursachen*
clothing	*Kleidung*
complain	*beklagen, Beschwerde einlegen*
complaint	*Beschwerde*
confidential	*vertraulich*
contain	*enthalten*
copper pipe	*Kupferrohr*
correspond	*entsprechen*
crate	*Kiste*
custom	*Kundschaft*
damaged	*beschädigt*
defective	*fehlerhaft, defekt*
demand	*Nachfrage*
disappointed	*enttäuscht*
discount	*Rabatt*
disposal; placed at the ~	*zur Verfügung gestellt*
dried dates	*getrocknete Datteln*
drive me round the bend	*mich verrückt machen*
elsewhere	*anderswo*
error	*Fehler*
fail to do	*etwas nicht tun, etwas unterlassen*
force	*zwingen*
going on (what is going on?)	*was ist los?*
grant	*gewähren*
importance	*Wichtigkeit*
inconvenience	*Unannehmlichkeit*

inspection	*Kontrolle*
instead of	*anstelle*
intend	*beabsichtigen*
item	*Artikel*
law; go to ~	*vor Gericht gehen*
let somebody have something	*jemandem etwas schicken*
look into	*prüfen*
make up	*Zusammensetzung*
matter	*Angelegenheit*
occur	*passieren*
overripe	*überreif*
oversight	*Versehen*
pick up	*abholen*
promote	*fördern*
punctuation	*Zeichensetzung*
recent	*neulich*
refund	*zurückzahlen*
regular	*regelmäßig*
reliable	*zuverlässig*
replacement	*Ersatz*
report	*berichten*
requirement	*Bedürfnis*
sample	*Muster*
settle	*erledigen, klären*
special delivery	*Sonderlieferung*
spelling	*Rechtschreibung*
spoilt	*verdorben*
store	*Lager*
stress	*betonen*
strictly	*streng*
surprised	*überrascht*
T-joint	*T-Stück*
take action	*etwas unternehmen*
terminate	*lösen*
to call attention to	*auf etwas aufmerksam machen*
upon; ~ opening	*bei (beim Öffnen)*

unable	*unfähig*
underweight	*untergewichtig*
waste	*verschwenden*
weigh	*wiegen*
wholesaler	*Großhändler*
with regard to	*hinsichtlich*

Put it ANOTHER WAY: Alternative phrases

Starting the letter	
we are forced to notify you ...	wir müssen Ihnen leider mitteilen
we are sorry that we must complain about ...	leider müssen wir ... reklamieren.
we feel forced to point out that ...	wir müssen darauf hinweisen, dass ...
Complaints	
crate no. 2 contains articles which we did not order	Kiste Nr. 2 enthält Artikel, die wir nicht bestellt haben
on/upon opening the box we found that it contained ...	beim Öffnen der Kiste stellten wir fest, dass ...
we cannot possibly accept these products as/because ...	wir können diese Waren unmöglich akzeptieren, da ...
it is clear that a mistake has been made	offensichtlich wurde ein Fehler gemacht
the goods were badly damaged when delivered	die Waren waren bei der Anlieferung schwer beschädigt
Ending the letter	
we must insist that ...	wir müssen darauf bestehen, dass ...
we look forward to your reply	wir erwarten Ihre Antwort
we hope that this error will not occur again	wir hoffen, dass ein solcher Fehler nicht wieder vorkommt

BRAIN WORK One: What's the English for...?

Translate the following German words into English.

1. reklamieren
2. darauf hinweisen
3. ich muss darauf bestehen, dass
4. vor Gericht gehen
5. beim Öffnen
6. Versehen
7. hinsichtlich

BRAIN WORK Two: Complete the letter

Over to you! Please put in the words below into the gaps in the letter.

inconvenience instead mistake point out as soon as upon

Dear Sirs

We are sorry to ... (**1**) ... that ... (**2**) ... opening crate no. 7 we found that a ... (**3**) ... had been made ... (**4**) ... of the twenty 10 kilo bags of Darjeeling tea, first quality, we received twenty 5 kilo bags.
This has caused us some ... (**5**) ...
Please let us have 100 extra kilos of the tea ... (**6**) .... possible.

Yours faithfully

BRAIN WORK Three: Quiz time

Please tick the correct answer and test your memory.

1. A customer may complain if:	**2.** "To reach a compromise" means here
a the goods are damaged	**a** seller and buyer go to law
b bills are paid	**b** seller and buyer make a deal
c the seller is polite	**c** the seller makes an error

3. If a seller refunds a buyer:

a the buyer gets money back
b the buyer gets replacements
c the seller says sorry

4. "I annulled the contract" This means:

a I lost the contract
b I cancelled the contract
c I wrote "0"on the contract

5. "The goods do not correspond to the quality ordered" means

a the products are not good enough
b the products are delayed
c the products are spoilt

6. If the seller sends the wrong quality the seller should:

a never admit the error
b admit the error
c invite the customer for lunch

BRAIN WORK Four: You construct a good letter

Here is a letter of complaint but the sentences are all mixed up.
Create a letter from them.

Crate no. 3 contained items, which were damaged and cannot be sold
Dear Sirs
We look forward to your prompt reply.
We regret to inform you that on receiving order number P8829 we were most disappointed.
Firstly crate no. 5 contained items that we did not order.
Yours faithfully
Clearly we must insist that these errors are rectified (*korrigiert*) as soon as possible.
Lastly crate no. 2 had parts missing (*fehlend*).
It is very clear that a mistake has been made.

CREDIT MATTERS

Chapter 15

Contents

Joke Time

Employee:	Can I have the day off[1] tomorrow to go Christmas shopping with my wife?
Boss:	You certainly can't, we are far too busy.
Employee:	Thank's a lot.

1 den Tag frei haben

FOCUS: Credit enquiries

In business it is normal for customers to ask for credit. The supplier must find out if the customer is creditworthy, especially if the supplier has not done business with the customer before. There are different ways to get information on a customer. A customer can supply trade references. This means that the customer gives the names of previous companies with whom business has been done. An alternative is that the customer gives the name of his or her bank. The customer can also provide information in the form recent balance sheets proving the solvency of his or her company. There are also so-called credit-enquiry agencies which can investigate a company's creditworthiness.
When someone writes to a firm asking for credit information this is confidential.
The letter may not have the name of the firm on it but the name of the firm is written on a separate slip of paper attatched to the letter. Reports on companies are usually cautious because of laws on libel and slander. If a firm does not give a report on a firm this is almost the same as giving a bad report.

DIALOGUE: How to put an enquiry about credit

Terry Jones (**TJ**) at Onions has been given the job of writing a letter to another firm to enquire about the creditworthiness of another company. Here he is talking to one of the secretaries, Helen Stevens (**HS**).

TJ: You know, I've got no idea at all about this. I mean I understand why we need to know if a firm can pay their bills on time but when I asked the boss about this he said that I should be 'cautious' about what I said and something about 'slander and libel law'.

HS: So what did you say then?

TJ: I'll read you what I wrote. 'Dear Sir, your name was given us by Stockman and Son. You have done business with them before, they said. Please ...' the boss said I should be polite as this is asking a favour.

Where was I? Oh yes 'Please tell us if they are solvent and if they pay on time. We are thinking about doing £10,000 of business with them. Thank you for your cooperation in this matter and we will treat the information confidentially' The last bit was the boss's idea, you know 'cooperation in this matter' and 'treat the blah, blah confidentially'. What do you think?

HS: Not bad apart from the fact that you shouldn't give the name in the letter.

TJ: What? How do they know who I'm talking about? I mean ...

HS: Hold on, hold on! You should write the name on a slip of paper and enclose it in the envelope. And the style could be better.

TJ: Okay, are you busy at the moment? Can you give me a few tips?

Drop Them A LINE: Onions ask for information

Here is the letter that Helen and Terry wrote:

Dear Sirs

Your name has been given to us by the firm mentioned on the slip attached. Would you please give us information with regard to the standing of the company and their reliability. Do you consider it safe to grant a credit of about £10,000?

We thank you very much for your cooperation and any information provided will be treated in the strictest confidence.

Yours faithfully

VOCABULARY: To help you understand

apart from	*abgesehen von*
balance sheet	*Bilanz*
cautious	*vorsichtig*
certainly not	*sicher nicht*

confidential	*vertraulich*
consider	*denken*
credit enquiry agency	*Kreditauskunftei*
creditworthiness	*Kreditwürdigkeit*
hold on!	*Moment mal!*
investigate	*überprüfen*
law	*Gesetz*
libel	*Verleumdung*
mention	*erwähnen*
previous	*vorherig, vorhergehend*
prove	*beweisen*
provide	*liefern*
recent	*neulich*
report	*Bericht, berichten*
slander	*Beleidigung*
slip of paper	*Blatt Papier*
solvency	*Zahlungsfähigkeit*
standing	*Ruf*
strictest	*strengst*
trade references	*Handelsreferenz*
treat	*behandeln*
with regard to	*in bezug auf*

Put It ANOTHER WAY: Alternative phrases

please let us have information about the firm	bitte geben Sie uns Auskünfte über die Firma
you were named as a reference	Sie wurden als Referenz genannt
as we have never done business with this firm before	da wir nie Geschäfte mit dieser Firma gemacht haben
as this firm is unknown to us	da wir diese Firma nicht kennen
please provide us with the usual trade reference	bitte geben Sie die üblichen Handelsreferenzen an
is the firm reliable and sound?	ist die Firma zuverlässig und solid?

we will treat the information with discretion	wir werden die Auskunft mit Verschwiegenheit behandeln
we hope we can be of assistance to you in a similar case	wir hoffen, daß wir Ihnen in einem ähnlichen Fall helfen können

BRAIN WORK One: Complete the letter

Please put in the words below into the letter and see what you can remember.

assistance consider reference information
slip reliable discretion grant

Dear Sirs

Private and Confidential
You have been named as a ... (**1**) ... by the firm mentioned on the ... (**2**) ... attached.
Please let us have ... (**3**) ... about the firm as we have never done business with them before. Is the firm ... (**4**) ... and sound? Do you ... (**5**) ... it safe to ... (**6**) ... a credit of about £12,000?
The information will be treated with ... (**7**) ...
We hope we can be of ... (**8**) ... in a similar case in future.

Yours faithfully

BRAIN WORK Two: Words from the chapter

Here are some words from the chapter with letters missing. Please put in the missing letters and give the German for the word.

1. p-evi-us	means in German ....?
2. st-n-ing	....?
3. r-cen-	....?
4. -olve-cy	....?
5. con-id-nt-a-	....?
6. cr-dit-ort-y	....?

BRAIN WORK Three: Quiz time

Over to you to see what you remember from 'Focus on credit enquiries'. Here are some questions about credit letters. Please say if they are true or false.

	T	F
1. It is important for a company to be creditworthy.		
2. It is not possible for a customer to prove her/ his creditworthiness.		
3. A credit-enquiry agency investigates the quality of goods.		
4. When you write to a firm asking about the creditworthyness of another company you should write the name, address and phone number of the firm clearly at the top of the page.		
5. A libel is a sort of bill.		
6. Solvent means that you can pay.		

LETTER BOX: When to use "date" and "appointment"

Date and appointment are two words that can cause confusion.

Date means Termin and Verabredung but also has the meaning of Rendezvous.

Appointment is more official. Normally it means a less official meeting.

For example "I have a date with my boyfriend."
Sometimes it is used loosely to mean something more official.
For example "Please arrange a date with the manager."

If it was clearly business you would use appointment.
You would not say "I have a date with the doctor."

Of course if the doctor was your boy or girlfriend then you could say date.

Look at this joke as an example

Sales representative: "I've been trying to see you for a week. Can we arrange to see each other some time next week?"
Boss of firm: "Please arrange a date with Miss Noden, my secretary."
Sales representative: "Well, I did and we had a very good time but I still need to see you to discuss business."

BRAIN WORK Four: Finding and correcting mistakes

The following letter contains seven mistakes. Please correct them.

Dear Sirs

The company mention on the slip attached have given your name to us. Could you please let us had information regarding the credit standing of the firm? Did you consider it safe to grants a credit of about £25,000?
We wish to thanking you very much for your co-operation and any information provided was be treated in the strictest confidence.

Yours faithfully

BRAIN WORK Five: A little more translation work

Translate the following sentences into English.

1. Sie wurden als Referenz genannt.
2. Die Firma ist zuverlässig und solide.
3. Können Sie uns Auskünfte über diese Firma geben?
4. Man sollte die Auskunft mit Verschwiegenheit behandeln.
5. Ich hoffe, dass ich Ihnen in einem ähnlichen Fall helfen kann.

16 Chapter

FAIRS AND EXHIBITIONS

Contents

Joke Time

Bob Onion: So Gerry, did you decide[1] anything important at the conference in Bermuda last week?
Salesman: Actually yes. We decided to have another conference there next month.

Two representatives[2] on the way to a trade fair in Bradford are talking on the train.

First rep: Have you been to the fair very often? It's my first visit.
Second: Actually[3] I've been here every year since 1986.
First: And what hotel would you recommend?[4] I hope I can still get a room.
Second: Try the Station Hotel.
First: Oh, have you stayed there before?
Second: No, never, but I've stayed in all the others.

1 beschließen 2 Vertreter 3 eigentlich 4 empfehlen

FOCUS: The role of trade fairs and exhibitions

Trade fairs and exhibitions are very important for passing on information and ideas. Normally they are only for business people and a lot of business is generated at fairs. Fairs and exhibitions specialize in one area or they may have a variety of products on display.

DIALOGUE: Onions discuss participation at a trade fair

Bob Onion (**BO**), the boss, Ian Miller (**IM**) and Gerry Murry (**GM**) from sales are planning taking part at a trade fair for heating equipment and other engineering products in Frankfurt.

BO: This will cost a lot of money but we need to try to get ourselves a name on the continent.
IM: And at the same time see what the competition is doing over there.
BO: You two need to go and take two engineers.
GM: And what about a secretary?
BO: Four people will be expensive enough with hotel costs, cost of a stand or booth. What do you need your secretary for?
GM: In case I need to write letters and somebody to take short hand.
BO: Total rubbish! You can leave the letter writing until you come back.
GM: Ah, well, Miss Brahms speaks very good German and we are all hopeless at foreign languages.
BO: Luckily one of the new engineers who is coming with you speaks German.
GM: I suppose he's some big hairy rugby type.
BO: Actually, he's a she. In fact both engineers are 'shes'.
GM: Oh well, that's different.
BO: Really. Well I want you to write a letter to reserve a good spot in the hall.

Drop Them A LINE: Onions ask about a trade fair in Frankfurt

Now take a look at the letter sent by Onions to the organisers of Heating 1997 Trade Fair:

Dear Sirs

We have had our attention drawn to your trade fair in Frankfurt, dates 14th to 20th October of this coming year.
Our firm, based in Birmingham in UK, develops and produces equipment for the heating engineering industry.
As we wish to make contact with customers in Europe, participation at your trade fair would be an ideal opportunity for us to meet people in our field in Germany.
Could you please forward us details including information about the cost of renting exhibition space and the conditions for taking part.

Your faithfully
Ian Miller

VOCABULARY: To help you understand

attention (draw attention to something)	*Aufmerksamkeit (auf etwas lenken)*
booth	*Stand*
competition	*Konkurrenz*
Continent	*Kontinentaleuropa*
dates ... to ...	*vom ... bis zum ...*
display (on display)	*Ausstellung (ausgestellt sein)*
equipment	*Ausrüstung*
exhibition	*Ausstellung*
foreign language	*Fremdsprache*
forward	*senden*
generate (be generated)	*entstehen*

get a name	*bekannt werden*
hairy	*haarig*
hopeless	*hoffnungslos*
including	*einschließlich*
opportunity	*Möglichkeit*
participate	*teilnehmen*
participation	*Teilnahme*
rent	*mieten*
shorthand	*Kurzschrift*
spot	*Stelle*
stand	*Stand*
suppose	*annehmen, vermuten*
take part	*teilnehmen*
toy	*Spielzeug*
trade fair	*Handelsmesse*
variety	*Vielfalt, Auswahl*

To Put It ANOTHER WAY: Alternative phrases

we wish to exhibit our goods at the fair	wir möchten unsere Waren auf der Messe ausstellen
we wish to organize/stage an exhibition	wir möchten eine Ausstellung veranstalten
is it still possible to rent/book exhibition space?	ist es noch möglich, Ausstellungsfläche zu mieten?
I wish to apply for space at a fair	ich möchte mich um Ausstellungsfläche bewerben
when is the deadline for applications?	wann ist Anmeldeschluss?
will the fees be refunded?	werden die Gebühren zurückerstattet?
we wish to cancel/withdraw our application	wir möchten unsere Anmeldung zurückziehen

when can we put up our stand?	wann können wir unseren Stand aufstellen?
when must we remove / dismantle our stand?	wann müssen wir unseren Stand abbauen?
our catalogues will be available to the visiting buyers	unsere Kataloge werden dem Käuferpublikum zur Verfügung stehen

BRAIN WORK One: Test your memory

And now put together the English and German words.

1. exhibition	a Möglichkeit
2. participate	b Handelsmesse
3. including	c Ausstellung
4. variety	d einschließlich
5. opportunity	e Vielfalt / Auswahl
6. trade fair	f teilnehmen

BRAIN WORK Two: Complete the letter

Please complete the letter below using the phrases and words from this chapter. Here are the words to help you. Good luck!

forward attention exhibited cancel space staged deadline fees

Dear Sirs

Last week our ... (**1**) ... was drawn to the trade fair, International Games and Toys Fair 20.. , which will be ... (**2**) ... by you in Dublin.
We are producers of high quality mechanical and electrical toys with our main factory near York.
As this is the first time we have ... (**3**) ... our goods at your fair we would like some information.

When is the ... (**4**) ... for applications? We hope that we are not too late and it is still possible to rent exhibition ... (**5**) ...?
If we wish to ... (**6**) ... our application will all the ... (**7**) ... be refunded?
Could you please ... (**8**) ... details including the cost of a small stand for 4 days?

Your faithfully

BRAIN WORK Three: Quiz time

Now a small quiz on the chapter.

1. Trade fairs are normally for: **a** business people only **b** all people **c** engineers	**2.** "Stage a fair" means: **a** cancel a fair **b** organize a fair **c** rent space at a fair
3. The German for "participate" is: **a** ausstellen **b** annehmen **c** teilnehmen	**4.** At a trade fair I would expect to see: **a** stands **b** check-in desks **c** a football match
5. Which is correct? **a** My attention was drawn to ... **b** My attention was pulled to ... **c** My attention was linked to ...	**6.** A "deadline" is: **a** A time after which a person dies **b** A train line that is not used **c** A last possible date or time

BRAIN WORK Four: You construct a letter

Here are some sentences about fairs and exhibitions but the words are mixed up. Make some good sentences.

1. at exhibit we would like to our products the fair
2. us deadline please tell the for applications the

3. our stand we by Friday must remove
4. we cancel our can application?
5. refund we the fees will
6. you on Monday up your stand can put

BRAIN WORK Five: How much do you understand?

Read the letter and answer the questions.

Dear Sirs

We saw on the Internet that you are organising a trade fair 'Medical Products International' in Birmingham between 12th July and 18th July.
We are a firm based in Bombay where we design and build wheel chairs. This is a new field for us as prior to this we built electrical motors for lifts and cranes.
We need to make ourselves known to the European market where we are sure that there is a ready market for our robust yet competitively priced products. So a stand at your fair would help us to break into the European market.
We also noted that you are running a number of two-day seminars to promote exhibitors' products at a number of venues (*Treffpunkte*) around the country prior to the trade fair.
Could you please forward us details including information about the seminars, cost of exhibition space and conditions of participation.

Yours faithfully
Navdeep Kang

1. Where did Mr Kang learn about the trade fair?
2. Instead of 'before' Mr Kang uses another word. What is this word?
3. What does Mr Kang's firm build?
4. How does he say 'conditions for taking part'?
5. What did Mr Kang's firm build?
6. Mr Kang uses a word for 'advertise / make known'. What is it?

BANKING

Chapter 17

Contents

FOCUS: Banks and banking
DIALOGUE: At Greyfellows Bank
DROP THEM A LINE: Letters about overdrafts
PUT IT ANOTHER WAY: Alternative phrases
BRAIN WORK: Complete a letter and make a memory test

Joke Time

My uncle who had overdrawn[1] his account[2] by too much received a sarcastic[3] letter from his bank manager.

Dear Mr Hemming

I have noticed that your account is now overdrawn well over the limit[4] and has been for some time. Can we please return to the original arrangement where you bank with us and not we bank with you?

Yours sincerely

The son of a business man was asked at school by the teacher:
"If your father borrowed[5] £50,000 from his bank and agreed to pay £5,000 of the loan[6] back every month, how much would he have paid after eight months?"
"£5,000."
"You don't know much about mathematics, Barry, do you?"
"And you don't know much about my father."

1 überzogen 2 Konto 3 sarkastisch 4 weit über das Limit 5 borgen 6 Darlehen

FOCUS: Banks and Banking

Banking performs a number of vital services both for the general public and business. For most people banks accept deposits, in other words you pay in money and the bank keeps it. The two main types of account are savings account and current account. The savings account is for people who want to save money and have an account that pays them a higher rate of interest. However, the money cannot be taken out or withdrawn as easily as with a current account. Almost all people and all businesses have a current account. It is very flexible as money is always at the customer's disposal. Bills can be paid by cheque, transfer, direct debit and standing order. More importantly the customer can borrow money. This credit can be a loan or overdraft. The bank will usually require some type of security for this. Banks are also important for helping to advise customers on the creditworthiness of firms, and paying bills from other countries and helping with various aspects of foreign trade.

DIALOGUE: At Greyfellows Bank

Greyfellows is a nation-wide bank in Britain. It is Onions' bank. Well, Onions do not own it but banks there. Here Miss Babcock (**B**) from the lending department is talking to Mr Stuffy (**S**), the manager:

B: Well, Mr Stuffy, I must say that I think we should contact Onion about the level of his overdraft. His facility is £700 per month but he is £1500 in the red.

S: Is that young Onion or old Onion?

B: I'm afraid it's young Onion, and we have already written to him threatening to withdraw his credit facility.

S: Miss Babcock! You can't possibly threaten our customers, especially an old trusted and reliable firm like Onions, and especially as I know old Mr Onion personally. I was at school with him you know ... or was it his father? Whatever, we don't threaten, oh no! We advise our customers.

B: Still, I do think we must take some action. I'll send a firm letter asking when he intends to get his overdraft in order. Unless you want to talk to his father personally at the golf course that is?

S: Er, pardon? I'll ignore that remark, Miss Babcock. Whatever you young types think, the old personal contact is still important.

B: I'll write a really firm letter then.

Drop Them A LINE: Letters about overdraft

Greyfellows bank sends a letter to young Onion:

Dear Mr Onion 21st February 20..

It has come to our attention that your account is overdrawn by £1,704.54 pence.
This is despite the fact that your originally agreed facility was well under half that, £700 to be precise. It is also despite the fact that we wrote to you on two previous occasions, 12th December 20.. and 24th January 20.., asking you to explain the reason for the delay in putting your account in the black.
Since then we have heard nothing. In fact the account was further overdrawn. If we do not hear from you within seven days we are forced to advise you that your credit facility will be suspended, and your account frozen. We regret having to take this action but the lack of response means that we have no choice.

Yours sincerely
Miss Tracy Babcock
Lending Department

Barry Onion writes back:

Dear Miss Babcock

It was with great surprise that I received your letter of 21st February 20.. . The delay in my replying to your letters before is that I was very ill with a tropical disease in the small African country, Twinanda, where I was doing voluntary work for a well-known charity.

You may wonder why the account was overdrawn due to a cheque paying £1305 to a travel agent Short's Caribbean Cruisers Ltd. when I was in Africa. The answer is simply that it was a poor relative's birthday, my old aunty Mavis, so I paid for her holiday.
You may also notice £206 withdrawn from my account direct debit at Guppy's Diving Equipment Shop. This is due to my aunty being a keen swimmer even though she is eighty five.
The overdraft will be cleared within the next few days from my father's account.

Yours sincerely
Barry Onion

VOCABULARY: To help you understand

account	*Konto*
advise	*verständigen, unterrichten, beraten*
attention; it has come to our ~	*wir sind darauf aufmerksam geworden*
banking	*Bankwesen*
charity	*Wohltätigkeitsverein*
clear	*begleichen*
credit facility	*Kreditrahmen*
current account	*laufendes Konto*
deposit	*deponieren, Einlage, Guthaben*
despite the fact that	*trotz der Tatsache, dass*
direct debit	*Einzugsermächtigung*
disposal; at my disposal ~	*Verfügung; zu meiner ~*
diving equipment	*Tauchgeräte*
facility	*Einrichtung, Möglichkeit*
firm	*streng, bestimmt*
frozen	*blockiert*
general public	*Publikum, Öffentlichkeit*

intend	*beabsichtigen*
interest (rate of interest)	*Zinsen (Zinssatz)*
in the black	*in den schwarzen Zahlen*
in the red	*in den roten Zahlen*
keen on	*stark interessiert an*
lending department	*Kreditabteilung*
level	*Ebene*
loan	*Darlehen*
occasion	*Mal, Gelegenheit*
overdraft	*Überziehung*
overdraw	*überziehen*
perform	*leisten, durchführen*
precise	*genau*
previous	*vorherig*
rate	*Satz, Kurs*
relative	*Verwandte*
remark	*Bemerkung*
require	*benötigen, erfordern*
savings account	*Sparkonto*
security	*Sicherheit*
service	*Dienstleistung*
standing order	*Dauerauftrag*
surprise	*überraschen*
suspend an account	*sperren; ein Konto ~*
take action	*Schritte unternehmen*
threaten	*drohen*
transfer	*überweisen*
tropical disease	*tropische Krankheit*
trusted	*vertrauenswürdig*
vital	*lebenswichtig*
voluntary work	*freiwillige Arbeit*
whatever	*wie auch immer*
withdraw	*abheben*

Put It ANOTHER WAY: Alternative phrases

please open / close account No ...	bitte eröffnen Sie / lösen Sie auf Konto Nr. ...
we would be pleased if you would arrange a credit of ...	wir wären dankbar, wenn Sie uns einen Kredit von ... gewähren würden
please allow us a loan of £20,000 for a period of 6 months	gewähren Sie uns bitte ein Darlehen von £20,000 für die Zeit von 6 Monaten
we need a loan as ...	wir brauchen ein Darlehen, weil ...
as security we wish to offer you	als Sicherheit können wir Ihnen bieten
I would be ready to call at the bank and discuss the matter	ich wäre gern bereit, Sie in der Bank aufzusuchen, um die Sache zu besprechen

BRAIN WORK One: Complete the letter

Over to you! Please complete the following letter asking for a loan by replacing the German words with English ones.

Dear Sir

We are writing to ask *Sie uns ein Darlehen von £20,000 für 12 Monate zu gewähren.*
Wir brauchen das Darlehen to buy new machines for our factory. We are sure that as *Kunden* of many years you will agree we are a creditworthy company.
Als Sicherheit können wir Ihnen bieten share certificates worth £25,000.
If you wish to discuss the *Sache, wäre ich gern bereit* to visit you *in der Bank.*

Yours faithfully

BRAIN WORK Two: Memory test

Take a try at completing these words from the chapter and then give the German word.

1. ov-rdr-f-	means in German	....?
2. ac-o-nt		....?
3. cu-r-nt acc-un-		....?
4. t-ansf-r		....?
5. l-an		....?
6. ch-q-e		....?

BRAIN WORK Three: Word power building

Here are six definitions and eight words / phrases. Put the correct words / phrases with the definition.

1. If you are .... it means you have less than zero in the bank.
2. To .... money means to move it from one account to another.
3. When I say .... money I mean put it in an account for example.
4. I could not use an account, which was ....
5. A .... is a system where the bank pays any regular / monthly bills for you.
6. If a bank gives me a .... I must pay the money back within a certain time.

frozen   transfer   standing order   loan   in the red   deposit

18 Chapter

APPLYING FOR A JOB

Contents

FOCUS: Job application types
DIALOGUE: In the personnel department
DROP THEM A LINE: A curriculum vitae and two covering letters
PUT IT ANOTHER WAY: Alternative phrases
BRAIN WORK: A little translation, correcting and constructing letters

Joke Time

The boss of the accounts[1] department at Onions, Barry White, was interviewing a young woman for the post as his private secretary. To show him that she was intelligent and a quick thinker she said: "One of my main interests is doing really difficult crossword puzzles[2]. I have even won prizes."
"Really, that's most interesting," said White, "but you see I'm looking for someone who is intelligent and on the ball[3] during office hours."
"Oh," said the candidate, "but that was in office hours!"

1 Buchführung 2 Kreuzworträtsel 3 auf Zack sein

FOCUS: Job application types

There are two types of written job application. The first is the solicited application. This is a letter in response to an advertisement in the press found in the section called 'situations vacant'. The second type is called the unsolicited application. Such applications are sent on the chance of a vacancy, often on the advice of a friend. Some people would call this 'applying on spec'.
A very important part of the application is the CV or curriculum vitae. This has all the details about the applicant including education, training and relevant experience. Sometimes copies of certificates must be submitted. Some firms and organisations ask applicants to fill in or complete special application forms.

DIALOGUE: In the personnel department

In Onions, Sue Onion (**SO**), the boss's daughter, has started work in the personnel department. Here she is talking to Judy James (**JJ**), the head of the department, about today's work.

JJ: Well, Sue, today we are going to look at those applications for the job we advertised in last Friday's 'Birmingham Globe'. The first thing to do is take a look at the curriculum vitae to see if the applicants have the minimum qualifications, then we'll weed out the untidy ones with spelling mistakes in the covering letter.

SO: So, I'll look at the, er cur ..., cura vita ..., curious vitals, and check on the exams the applicants passed?

JJ: Curriculum vitae! Curriculum vitae!

SO: Sorry, I was never very good at French. Anyway, the CV.

JJ: Yes, and then take a look at the letters. Think about your own application and how you would write it. You know that the application is the first impression that we get so presentation is as important as the candidate's qualifications.

SO: Could I take a look at a CV and some letters and you tell me what is good and what isn't so good? You see I didn't write a covering letter.

JJ: You mean you filled in an application form?

SO: Well, my dad filled it in for me and only my name and address.

JJ: I see. Well, take a look at this good CV and two letters. One is too informal and the other is okay. You tell me which is best.

Drop Them A LINE: A curriculum vitae and two covering letters

Curriculum vitae

Name:	Julius Eric Cheeser	
Address:	16 Beechhill Road, Sheffield, Yorkshire, S10 2SB	
Telephone:	(0742) 683375	
Date of Birth:	11th July, 1965	
Education:		
1972 to 1983	King Edward's High School GCE "O" Level 8 passes "A" Level 3 passes	
Work Experience:		
1984 to 1989	Employer: Turner and Walker, Engineering Ltd, 25 Ringinglow Road, Sheffield W45 5DT	Duties: Trainee Accountant
1989 to 1996	Valiant Insurance, 46 Queen's Road, Sheffield T7F 3BB	Duties: Clerk, Account's Department

Special Interests: Ice skating, football, reading, music

References: Mrs. Martin, General Manager, Valiant Insurance, 46 Queen's Road Sheffield T7F 3BB

Mr. Turner, Partner, Turner and Walker Engineering Ltd., Ringinglow Road, Sheffield W45 5DT

Take a look at these two covering letters, the first is written in a poor style, the second is acceptable:

Dear Mrs James

I saw a job that you advertised in the newspaper last week. The job was for a clerk in the accounts department with your company.
I want to apply for the job because I'm very interested in this type of work and I have already trained to do such a job and I have over 3 years experience as you can see from my CV in a good firm that does the same kind of work as yours.
I think I would be good at the job because of what I have said and it would be good to work with a good company like yours. The money and holidays are also good.
If you want I can see you at an interview

Yours sincerely
Tom Grossly

Dear Mrs James

I wish to be taken into consideration as an applicant for the post of clerk in your accounts department, as advertised in the Birmingham Globe dated 12th April 20.. .
The reason for my application for the position is that I have in excess of three years experience employed by a company involved in the same area as Onions Ltd. As a result I am sure that I can contribute positively to your company. I would also be extremely keen to work for a well-established and respected firm such as yours. As can be seen from my CV I am fully qualified as an accounting clerk.
You will see that I give the names of two referees who will be happy to vouch for my abilities at work.
I would be pleased to have the opportunity of discussing my candidature with you at an interview.
Please do not hesitate to contact me if you have any queries regarding this application.

Yours sincerely
Martin Smart

VOCABULARY: To help you understand

ability	*Fähigkeit*
accountant	*Buchhalter*
accounts department	*Buchhaltungsabteilung*
advertise	*annoncieren*
advertisement	*Anzeige, Annonce*
applicant	*Bewerber*
application	*Bewerbung*
apply for	*bewerben um*
apply on spec	*sich auf gut Glück bewerben*
area	*Gebiet*
candidature	*Kandidatur*
certificate	*Zeugnis*
complete a form	*ein Formular ausfüllen*
consideration; take into ~	*in Betracht ziehen*
contribute	*beitragen*
covering letter	*Begleitbrief*
curious	*neugierig*
curriculum vitae (CV)	*Lebenslauf*
dated	*datiert*
duty	*Pflicht*
education	*Ausbildung*
employed	*beschäftigt sein*
employee	*Arbeitnehmer*
excess; in excess ~ of	*über (mehr als)*
experience	*Erfahrung*
fill in / complete	*ausfüllen*
form	*Formular*
GCE A Level	*Abitur*
GCE O Level	*mittlere Reife*
hesitate	*zögern*
ice skating	*Eislauf*
impression	*Eindruck*
interview	*Vorstellungsgespräch*

involved	*beteiligt*
keen	*sehr interessiert*
post	*Stelle*
query	*Frage*
referee	*Referenz*
reference	*Referenz (Zeugnis)*
regarding	*in bezug auf*
respected	*angesehen*
response; in ~ to	*in Antwort auf*
situations vacant	*Stellenangebote*
spelling mistake	*Rechtschreibfehler*
submit	*einreichen*
untidy	*unordentlich*
vacancy	*freie Stelle*
vitals	*lebenswichtige Organe*
vouch for	*sich verbürgen für*
weed out	*aussieben*
well established	*gut eingeführt*

Put It ANOTHER WAY

I should like to apply for the position as ...	Ich möchte mich um die Stelle als ... bewerben
please consider my application for the position as ...	Bitte ziehen Sie meine Bewerbung für die Stelle als ... in Betracht
I have been told that there is a vacancy in your department	ich habe erfahren, dass in Ihrer Abteilung eine Stelle frei ist
I am writing to enquire if you have an opening for a secretary	hiermit möchte ich anfragen, ob Sie eine freie Stelle für eine Sekretärin haben
I enclose my curriculum vitae as well as copies of certificates	ich füge meinen Lebenslauf sowie Kopien von Zeugnissen bei

at present I am employed as ... with Johnson Ltd.	augenblicklich bin ich als ... bei Johnson Ltd beschäftigt
the reason for my application is ...	der Grund für diese Bewerbung ist ...
I wish to work in a post with more responsibility	ich möchte eine Stelle mit mehr Verantwortung haben
I would like to widen my experiences and improve my prospects for promotion	ich möchte meine Erfahrungen erweitern und meine Aussichten auf Beförderung verbessern
I am at present unemployed	augenblicklich bin ich arbeitslos
my previous employer is willing to provide a reference for me	mein früherer Arbeitgeber ist bereit, eine Empfehlung für mich zu geben
I would be grateful if you sent me an application form	ich wäre dankbar, wenn Sie mir ein Bewerbungsformular schicken würden
I will be happy to attend an interview	ich würde gerne zu einem Vorstellungsgespräch kommen
I am available for interview by arrangement	ich bin für ein Vorstellungsgespräch nach Vereinbarung verfügbar
I look forward to hearing a positive reply from you	ich würde mich über eine positive Antwort freuen
I will be pleased to send any further information you may request	ich schicke Ihnen gern jede gewünschte Information

BRAIN WORK One: A little translation work

Here is a covering letter but unfortunately the person writing it left some of it in German. Please try and translate the German into English. Use the phrases and vocabulary in this chapter to help you.

Dear Mrs Duffy

Ich möchte mich um die Stelle bewerben as accountant which was advertised in the Daily Echo dated 23rd November 19.. .
As you can see from my curriculum vitae *bin ich augenblicklich als Buchhalter bei Humble and Thwackit beschäftigt.*
Although I am happy here, *ich möchte eine Stelle mit mehr Verantwortung haben*. I would also like to widen my experiences *und meine Aussichten auf Beförderung verbessern.*
I will be pleased to send you *weitere* information and *ich bin für ein Vorstellungsgespräch nach Vereinbarung verfügbar.*
I look forward to receiving a positive reply from you.

Yours sincerely
Victoria Hope

BRAIN WORK Two: Correct the spelling mistakes

Over to you. Have a try at correcting the spelling mistakes and typing errors in the application below. You or the secretary have had a really bad day. Here is a tip: there are twelve mistakes. Oh, and another tip: some of the mistakes are typically German!

Dear Sir

I would like you to take me into consideration vor the position of engineer in your engineering deplartmint , as advertised in the Birmingham Globe, dited 23rd March 20.. .
The reason for my ablikation are that I have many years experience in this area and I am sure that I can positively contribute to your company.
I am very clean to work for your company which is very well established and respkted.
You will see that I give the names of two rfreees who will be happy to wouch for my abilities at work. I would be pleased to have the oppertuniti to discuss my candidature with you at an interwiew.
Blease do not hesitate to kontakt me if you have any queries rigardink this application.

Yours faithfully

BRAIN WORK Three: Test your vocabulary

Put the German words together with the words in English.

1. in Bezug auf	a in response to
2. Bewerber	b education
3. Ausbildung	c applicant
4. in Antwort auf	d apply for
5. bewerben um	e vacancy
6. freie Stelle	f regarding

BRAIN WORK Four: You construct a letter

Here are some typical phrases used when applying for a job. Sorry but they are mixed up. Please put them in order to make good sentences.

1. the post apply of I wish to for teacher.
2. I interview will happy to be attend an.
3. at employed present I am in the accounts Peabody & Sons department at.
4. to work in a position more with responsibility I would like.
5. the main reason for application my is that I not do wish to work in evenings the.
6. the post consider my application for as receptionist please.

GOING INTERNATIONAL Chapter 19

GOING INTERNA-
TIONAL

Contents

Joke Time

One day Bob Onion noticed[1] that one of the secretaries had been making changes to letters he dictated[2].
"Miss Barnes, in future, please do what you are paid for and leave the thinking to me," said Onion and added "I would be most pleased if you wrote down exactly[3] what I said thank you."
Not long after a customer received a letter from Bob Onion and it went as follows: "Dear Mr Smythe – write that with a 'y' and stick[4] an 'e' at the end – the silly old idiot[5] thinks it makes him sound more important.
In response to your letter dated ... what was it? Oh look it up yourself will you. Anyway, we can offer you as our most respected and reliable[6] agent in Scotland – well, as far as we know, because we haven't noticed you swindling[7] us – a percentage of ... now how little can I offer him? 25%, no I'll try 15% and see if he says anything.
I hope this is acceptable – if not go jump in a lake[8].

Yours most sincerely blah blah blah."

1 bemerken 2 diktieren 3 genau 4 setzen 5 blöder alter Idiot 6 zuverlässig 7 betrügen 8 in einen See springen

FOCUS: Doing business through agents

Big companies have whole departments to deal with distribution and export of their products outside their domestic markets. Really large companies can produce in part or totally overseas through subsidiaries. Smaller companies will make use of agents who work for themselves, often for commission as a percentage of what they sell. Agents are useful because they are cheaper than employing people full time. They also know their own market and are familiar with local customs and are in a better position to do business in their own area.

DIALOGUE: Onions discuss agency agreements

Trying to expand into markets outside Britain has not been easy. The market for boilers and heating equipment is not saturated in Britain but Bob Onion (**BO**) is an ambitious boss and as he says "Don't put all your eggs in one basket". Here we find him talking to two of his sales managers, Gerry Murry (**GM**) and Ian Miller (**IM**)

BO: Sales have been good but I want to know about selling abroad.
IM: We just don't know local conditions in a lot of countries.
BO: Exactly, for example what about that agent in Jamaica? Williams was it? Mr Murry, you sent him £540 worth of heating equipment on a trial basis. Since then how much has he sold?
GM: She sir, I mean he is a she. He's, I mean, she's called Mrs Williams not Mr Will ...
BO: I don't care if he was an 'it', Mr or Mrs! How many pounds of business have we had?
GM: From Mrs Williams, in Jamaica?
BO: Yes, from Mrs Williams in Jamaica!
GM: Er, so far?
BO: Yes, since we sent the heating equipment after you met Mrs Williams at the trade fair in, eh, in the Bahamas, yes the Bahamas, wasn't it?
GM: In pounds?
BO: Yes, in pounds!

GM: None. She seemed very professional. It was all about chicken farms and since a lot of people eat chicken in Jamaica the demand for heating equipment in the hatcheries should be massive.

IM: May I make a suggestion? We had a lot of interest at the Frankfurt Trade Fair. How about contacting Chambers of Commerce in Germany and asking them to put us in touch with reliable companies that can market our equipment there? Oh yes, and we had a lot enquiries from that Chinese company that said they thought our equipment would sell well in China.

BO: At last, a sensible suggestion! Get the addresses and write letters straight away!

Drop Them A LINE: Getting help from Chambers of Industry and Commerce

Dear Sirs

Our company produces a wide range of heating units suitable for home and industrial use. Please find enclosed illustrated literature describing our products.
So far we have mostly sold our equipment on the domestic market and to a limited extent in Russia. Due to our success we consider we would also find a ready market in your country.
We are now seeking agents to sell our products on your market.
The agent must be reliable and have considerable experience in marketing such products.
We would be very grateful if you could assist us in getting in touch with suitable and reputable businesses.

Your faithfully
Ian Miller

Not much later Onions received a reply to their letter from Germany:

Dear Mr Miller

The local Chamber of Industry and Commerce was kind enough to supply us with your address and literature describing the various types of heating units produced by your firm.
Our company is a leading importer and distributor of boilers and heating equipment of many years standing. As a consequence we have valuable connections in the trade and a small but experienced team of sales staff.
We have looked at your brochures and are convinced that there is a promising market waiting to be developed here. Can you please contact us to detail the terms on which you want us to represent you.
If your firm is prepared to grant us the agency we will spare no effort to promote the sale of your product.

Yours sincerely
Fritz Gruber

V VOCABULARY: To help you understand

agency agreement	*Vertretervertrag*
agent	*Vertreter*
appoint	*ernennen*
appreciate	*zu schätzen wissen*
appreciative	*dankbar*
Chamber of Industry and Commerce	*Industrie- und Handelskammer*
consequence; as a ~	*als Folge*
consider	*betrachten*
considerable	*beträchtlich*
demand	*Nachfrage*
develop a market	*einen Markt erschließen*
distribution	*Verteilung*
distributor	*Großhändler*
domestic market	*Binnenmarkt*
due to	*aufgrund, wegen*

experience	*Erfahrung*
experienced	*erfahren*
furnish with something	*mit etwas versorgen*
grant an agency	*eine Vertretung übertragen*
grateful	*dankbar*
hatcheries	*Hühnerfarm*
hold the view that	*der Ansicht sein*
illustrated literature	*Bildmaterial*
keen on	*stark interessiert an*
leading	*führend, wichtig*
line	*Branche*
locate something	*etwas finden*
market a product	*etwas auf den Markt bringen*
opinion; be of the ~	*der Meinung sein*
overseas market	*Überseemarkt*
owing to	*infolge*
promote	*fördern*
prospect	*Aussicht*
provide with	*mit etwas versorgen*
put in touch / contact	*in Verbindung setzen*
range	*Sortiment, Auswahl*
ready market; find a ~	*einen guten Markt finden*
reliable	*zuverlässig*
reputable	*seriös, solide*
response; in ~ to your letter	*in Beantwortung Ihres Briefes*
result; as a ~	*als Folge*
saturated	*gesättigt*
spare no effort	*keine Mühe scheuen*
standing; of many years' ~	*mit einem langjährigen guten Ruf*
subsidiary	*Tochtergesellschaft*
success	*Erfolg*
suitable	*geeignet*
supply	*beliefern*
thorough	*gründlich*
trade	*Handel, Geschäft*
valuable	*wertvoll*
wide range	*große Auswahl*

Put it ANOTHER WAY: Alternative phrases

if you are not already represented here we would be interested in ...	falls Sie hier noch keine Vertretung haben, wären wir interessiert ...
we have acted as agents for Messrs ... for many years	wir waren viele Jahre als Agenten für die Firma ... tätig
with more than 20 years experience	mit einer Erfahrung von mehr als 20 Jahren
we have a thorough knowledge of the market	wir haben eine gründliche Marktkenntnis
we will increase our activities in the near future	wir werden unsere Tätigkeiten in der nahen Zukunft erweitern
we have branches in all major cities	wir haben Filialen in allen großen Städten
we wish to act as a sole agent	wir möchten als Alleinvertreter tätig sein
we already represent five leading companies	wir vertreten schon fünf führende Firmen
we have specialised in selling ...	wir sind auf den Verkauf von ... spezialisiert
we feel sure that we will have a successful relationship	wir sind sicher, dass wir eine erfolgreiche Geschäftsbeziehung haben werden

BRAIN WORK One: Pick out the correct word

Have a try at the following Brain Work and put in one of the three possibilities to complete the sentences correctly.

branches relationships leading

1. The company has ... in all large cities

team | sole agent | opportunists

2. We wish to act as your ... here in Italy

electrical | valuable | detailed

3. This agency has ... connections in this line

leading | distributed | experienced

4. Our company is a / an ... importer of this equipment

sale | knowing | knowledge

5. We have a thorough ... of the local market

BRAIN WORK Two: Quiz time

Last but not least a small quiz on the chapter.

1. Agents are useful for:
   - a production
   - b selling
   - c banking

2. Agents are often paid:
   - a provisions
   - b commission
   - c deals

3. Knowledge of local markets is:
   - a reputable
   - b important for selling
   - c important for banking

4. Large firms can produce overseas in their:
   - a subsidiaries
   - b departments
   - c domestics

5. The English for "Erfolg" is:
   - a follow
   - b success
   - c experience

6. Another word for the home market is the:
   - a domestic market
   - b overseas market
   - c outside market

BRAIN WORK Three: How much can you understand?

Look at the letter and answer the questions on it. A Spanish retailer contacts a British firm to find out about becoming an agency.

Dear Sirs

Our firm is a major distributor of office furniture in Spain having outlets in all large cities including Barcelona, Madrid and Granada. We have been in business for the last twenty years and have valuable contacts in the business. We have looked at your web site and are convinced that there is a good market waiting to be developed here for your products.
Please contact us as soon as possible to give us the terms on which you wish us to act as your representative.
We are more than happy to provide references as we have worked happily and successfully for other British firms acting as their agents.
If your company is willing to grant us the agency we will do our utmost to further the sale of your products locally.
Yours faithfully

1. What does the Spanish firm do?
2. What word is used meaning 'shops'?
3. Does the Spanish firm only have three outlets?
4. Where did the Spanish firm find out about the British firm?
5. Has the Spanish firm worked with British firms before?
6. How does the Spanish firm say it will do its best to sell the British firm's products in Spain?

SHIPPING GOODS

Chapter 20

Contents

FOCUS: Transport and shipping
DIALOGUE: Onions arrange a shipment to China
DROP THEM A LINE: Advice of dispatch to Hong Kong
PUT IT ANOTHER WAY: Alternative phrases
BRAIN WORK: Translation time
LETTER BOX: A few prepositions
More **BRAIN WORK**: Test your prepositions and your error finding talent

Joke Time

Bob Onion met the boss of another company, Fred Potter, in the pub.
Onion: How's business?
Potter: Great! One of my people got an order for £160,000 last week.
Onion: £160,000! I just don't believe it!
Potter: It's totally true. Look, I've got the cancellation[1] right here.

1 Stornierung

FOCUS: Transport and shipping

Normally, details of how goods are to be shipped or forwarded are given in the order. For example details will be given on how the goods are packed. This depends on the type of goods and in part how the goods are transported. For example, perishable goods like food cannot be transported in the same way as machine parts, timber or coal. In the same way the means of transport is influenced by the type of goods, how soon the goods are needed and availability of cargo space. Clearly this can be a complex matter and is frequently put into the hands of specialists called forwarding agents and carriers. These people are very familiar with the problems of transport. They also get lower rates for shipping as they can send several different consignments together. They also provide shipping documents and arrange insurance and deal with customs. On the international level forwarding agents have offices in many countries and are easily in a position to transport goods efficiently.

DIALOGUE: Onions arrange a shipment to China

Gerry Murry (**GM**) and Ian Miller (**IM**) are looking at the options for sending their equipment overseas. They have found an agent in China and they have received an order for boilers from this agent.

GM: I wrote to a couple of shipowners asking for quotations for their freight rates from Liverpool to Hong Kong.

IM: Hong Kong, really?

GM: Yes, the agent wants the boilers sent to Hong Kong and then they will distribute them by truck or train to China. I have a reply here from one shipowner (*reads the letter*)

Dear Sirs, we have received your enquiry of 29th April and can inform you that our current freight rate for boilers in crates, Liverpool to Hong Kong is £55 per metric tonne. We sail once a week. Hong Kong is our last port of call and the voyage takes twenty one days. (*stops reading*)

Now, my question is "what did they say in the order, when did they say they needed the boilers?"

IM: In four weeks.

GM: That's okay then. They sent a sailing card for cargo ship Enterprise and a shipping instruction form. I'll fill it in and send it back.

Drop Them A LINE: Advice of despatch to Hong Kong

A week later Gerry Murry informs the customers that the order has been despatched:

Dear Sirs

Your Order No. 459/f of 3rd April 20..

We are pleased to inform you that the water heaters (boilers) ordered under the above order have been despatched as arranged.
The boilers are packed in 10 crates, 4 boilers to a crate. The crates are marked JGO in square, HONG KONG and are numbered 1–10.
The shipment is arriving in Hong Kong on 25th May, on the Enterprise, which sailed from Liverpool today.
Shipping document including bills of lading, commercial invoices, and insurance certificate, in triplicate have been sent together with our sight draft for £765, to Barclays Bank, Oxford St, in accordance with the letter of credit opened with them.
We are convinced that the boilers will prove to be satisfactory and we hope you will contact us again in the near future with new orders.

Yours faithfully
G. Murry.

VOCABULARY: To help you understand

accordance; in ~ with	*gemäß, entsprechend*
availability	*Vorrätigkeit*
cargo	*Fracht*

coal	*Kohle*
commercial invoice	*Handelsrechnung*
consignment	*Sendung*
convinced; to be ~	*sicher sein, überzeugt sein*
crate	*Kiste*
customs	*Zoll*
despatch	*versenden*
enquiry	*Anfrage*
familiar	*vertraut*
fill in	*ausfüllen*
food	*Nahrungsmittel*
form	*Formular*
forward	*befördern, senden*
forwarding agent	*Spediteur*
freight rate	*Frachtsatz*
influence	*beeinflussen*
insurance	*Versicherung*
insurance certificate	*Versicherungszertifikat*
letter of credit	*Akkreditiv*
mark	*beschriften*
matter	*Sache, Angelegenheit*
number	*nummerieren*
perishable	*leicht verderblich*
port of call	*Anlaufhafen*
rate	*Satz*
sail	*auslaufen*
ship	*verschiffen, versenden*
shipowner	*Reederei*
shipping documents	*Versanddokumente*
shipping instructions	*Versandanweisungen*
sight draft	*Sichtwechsel*
square	*Viereck*
timber	*Holz, Bauholz*
truck	*Lastwagen*

Put it ANOTHER WAY: Alternative Phrases

we want to charter a ship	wir möchten ein Schiff chartern
we need a ship with a cargo capacity of 5,000 tons	wir brauchen ein Schiff mit einer Ladekapazität von 5000 Tonnen
the ship must be ready for loading on 2nd November	das Schiff muß am 2. November ladebereit sein
we understand that you offer a global freight service	wir haben erfahren, dass Sie einen weltweiten Frachtdienst anbieten
your company operates a container service	Ihr Unternehmen unterhält einen Containerdienst
the goods will be packed in cartons	die Waren werden in Kartons verpackt
the cartons measure ... x ... x ...cm and weigh ... kg	Die Kartons haben die Abmessung ... x ... x ... cm und wiegen ... kg
please quote us your lowest rates	nennen Sie uns bitte Ihre niedrigs-tenTarife
please let us have the times and frequency of your sailings	bitte teilen Sie uns mit, wann und wie oft die Route gefahren wird
please tell us the name of the next ship sailing to Tripoli and the deadline for accepting cargo	bitte nennen Sie uns den Namen des nächsten Schiffes nach Tripolis und den letzten Termin, an dem Ladungen angenommen werden
please deliver the goods at once / not later than 4th march / by road / by air	bitte beförden Sie die Waren sofort / nicht später als 4. März / per Last-wagen / durch Luftfracht
please ensure the goods are not stored in the open	bitte sorgen Sie dafür, dass die Wa-ren nicht im Freien gelagert werden
our packing instructions must be strictly observed	unsere Packanweisungen müssen genau beachtet werden

BRAIN WORK One: Translate some parts

Over to you! Please translate the parts of the letter left in German by a lazy colleague! Use the phrases in this chapter to help you.

Dear Sirs

We have *erfahren, daß Ihre Firma einen Containerdienst unterhält.*
Our company needs to send 54 diesel motors to Istanbul and we would like a quotation for your current *Frachtsätze. Die Waren werden in Kisten verpackt und haben die Abmessung 1 Meter 50 cm x 1 Meter 20 x 2 Meter und wiegen 1258 kg.*
Please let us have the times and frequency of you sailings *und nennen den Namen des Schiffes und den letzten Termin, an dem Ladungen angenommen werden.*

Yours faithfully

LETTER BOX: A few prepositions

Prepositions are always tricky. Here are some of the more important ones used in business letter writing. Note that with certain nouns and verbs we use certain prepositions.

in response to your letter *in* reply to your letter	als Antwort auf Ihren Brief als Antwort auf Ihren Brief
on examining the shipment	bei der Untersuchung der Sendung
we are interested *in* this model	wir interessieren uns für dieses Modell
we must insist *on* prompt delivery	wir müssen auf prompter Lieferung bestehen
the shipment consisted *of* 4 crates	die Sendung bestand aus 4 Kisten
we waited two weeks *for* the goods	wir warteten zwei Wochen auf die Waren

he will pay *by* cheque or *in* cash	er wird in bar oder mit Scheck bezahlen
delivery *by* van	Lieferung durch Lieferwagen
with reference *to* our previous correspondence	unter Bezugnahme auf unsere vorhergehende Korrespondenz

BRAIN WORK Two: Test your prepositions

Time to see if you can put in the prepositions. Use the information from the letter box to put in the correct prepositions.

1. All bills will be paid ... cheque.
2. We are writing to you ... response to your letter dated 12 June 20.. .
3. Our company is very interested ... this product.
4. ... examining the crates we saw that two were damaged.
5. Delivery will be ... train.
6. ... reference to our previous letter, we wish to point out that delivery must be prompt.

BRAIN WORK Three: Sort out mixed up sentences

Here are some typical phrases in used when writing about shipping goods. They are all mixed up so make them into good English sentences.

1. wooden goods the will be packed in crates.
2. packing observe please the instructions.
3. we to charter a Lisbon ship to wish.
4. us please rates quote the lowest.
5. we will hire container a for our to move Qatar
6. flights let please us have the your times of.

BRAIN WORK Four: Test your error finding talent

Read the following letter and correct the ten mistakes. A firm informs the customer that the goods have been sent.

Dear Ms Katzer

We are most pleased to informing you that the ceramics have beer despatched as arranged. The pots have been packed in 21 woollen crates. The cakes are marked GD in a green square and are numbered 1 to 21. The shipment will arrive in Hull on 11th September on the Argo, which soiled from Gibraltar this mornig.
All shipping documents have bean sent to Barclays Bank in Halifax.
We are convinced that our ceramic goods will cell very well and we hop you will contract us in the near future with further orders.

Yours sincerely
A. Martinez

SUBSIDIARIES

Chapter 21

Contents

Joke Time

Onions is expanding. Bob Onion invited[1] five of his sales team into his office.
"You have all done so well with selling abroad that I'm giving you all a cheque for £1,500. If you keep working like this, I may even sign[2] it."

1 einladen 2 unterschreiben

FOCUS: Subsidiaries and branches

There are many advantages to having a branch or subsidiary abroad. Producing in a country close to the market means that you can reduce transport costs and all problems that can result from transporting goods. A subsidiary is a separate firm but its capital is controlled by the home company. A branch is part of the home company. Being close to a market also means you are more familiar with the needs of your customer, you know what they require and can change your product accordingly. You can avoid quotas and tariffs as your product is not imported. Depending on where a factory is set up, there are advantages with lower wages and lower costs in general. Local and national governments are willing to help with assistance such as cheap or even free factory space as well as financial incentives.

However, establishing a production facility in a foreign country can be risky and is very expensive because of the cost of investment.

DIALOGUE: Onions go to China

Bob Onion (**BO**) is talking to his main investor, Ted Cash (**TC**), and Ron Stuffy (**RS**) from Greyfellows Bank.

TC: The advantages are clear Bob, I can see that producing our boilers in China will be cheaper and there is a ready market there, but why China? It's so far away. And the risks!

BO: The sale of our boilers in China through our new agent in Hong Kong is, well, to be honest incredible. We just can't keep up with demand. You know we have transport costs and quotas to pay. Oh, and you haven't forgotten that little strike we had. Well, in the situation at the moment in a rapidly expanding market with lots of competition any hold up could be fatal. In China there will be no strike risk and no transport costs and no quotas.

RS: Yes, but there will be other costs. Massive investment.

BO: Do we have the money?

RS: Well yes, but ...
BO: There we are then!
TC: Not so fast, Bob! What about our sales in Germany and Eastern Europe? Didn't we sell a lot in Germany?
BO: We did, our equipment is cheap and efficient.
TC: So why not set up production there?
BO: You must be kidding! Think of the labour costs.
RS: Yes, according to our information it would cost 50% more to produce in Germany than even in Britain.
BO: What's more we have been told by our agent in Hong Kong that we will get a lot of help from the local government in Shanghai.
TC: Well, okay then. We will discuss this with other investors but I want to see on paper what's on offer and then we will go ahead.
BO: Great. I'll drop the ministry or council or whatever they are called in Shanghai a line to ask about what they can offer us.
TC: One other thing. I hope that this won't mean closing production here. This company has been making boilers here for years and it would sad to see all that change.
BO: Don't worry, demand here will stay high. Now, sorry gentlemen but I have a letter to write.

Drop Them A LINE: An enquiry about a subsidiary

Bob Onion writes a letter to the Shanghai City Council to enquire about setting up a production facility in Shanghai:

Dear Sirs

We have obtained your address from your embassy in London. Our company is an expanding engineering business active in the area of heating equipment and water boilers.
As demand for our products is expanding in the Far East we are evaluating the best location of such a plant to satisfy demand both in China but also in neighbouring countries.
At present we are doing a lot of business with your country on an agency

basis but demand is so great for our products that we are considering setting up a production plant in the Shanghai area. If conditions are positive we will look for a company there which will act as a joint owner of a subsidiary. We wish to establish a full production plant together with distribution and service facilities.
We would be very pleased if you would send us information on industrial sites in the Shanghai area together with financial assistance and other incentives.
We are looking forward to hearing from you soon.

Yours sincerely
Robert Onion
Managing Director

VOCABULARY: To help you understand

abroad	*im Ausland*
accordingly	*dementsprechend*
advantage	*Vorteil*
area	*Gebiet*
assistance	*Hilfe*
avoid	*vermeiden*
branch	*Filiale*
close to	*in der Nähe von*
condition	*Bedingung*
consider	*glauben*
council	*Verwaltung*
demand	*Nachfrage*
depending on	*hier: je nachdem*
distribution	*Verteilung*
embassy	*Botschaft*
establish	*gründen*
evaluate	*einschätzen, beurteilen*
expanding	*expandierend*

facility	*Einrichtung*
in general	*im allgemeinen*
incentive	*Anreiz*
incredible	*unglaublich*
inspect	*besichtigen*
joint owner	*Mitbesitzer*
local government	*Kommunalverwaltung*
location	*Lage, Örtlichkeit*
look for	*suchen nach*
ministry	*Ministerium*
need	*Bedürfnis*
neighbouring	*angrenzend, benachbart*
obtain	*bekommen, erhalten*
plant	*Anlage, Fabrik*
quota	*Kontingent*
satisfy	*zufriedenstellen*
set up	*gründen, einrichten*
site	*Gelände, Stelle, Grundstück*
space	*Platz, Raum*
subsidiary	*Tochtergesellschaft*
tariff	*Zoll*
transport cost	*Transportkosten*
wage	*Lohn*
willing to	*bereit zu*

Put It ANOTHER WAY: Alternative phrases

if you move your company here there will be several advantages	wenn Sie Ihre Firma hierher verlegen, bieten sich mehrere Vorteile
there are good road and rail connections	es gibt gute Straßen- und Bahnverbindungen
the government will provide incentives	die Regierung wird Anreize bieten

incentivessites are available for rent	Grundstücke können gepachtet werden
you can inspect the sites	Sie können die Grundstücke besichtigen
there are factory buildings available for immediate use	es gibt Fabriken, die zu sofortiger Nutzung zur Verfügung stehen
if you wish to expand your factory there will be no problem as there is building land adjoining	falls Sie Ihre Fabrik erweitern möchten, wird es kein Problem geben, da Bauplatz angrenzt
special loans are available	Sonderfinanzierungen werden gewährt

BRAIN WORK One: Memory work

Over to you! Test your memory and see if can put the German and English words together

1.	subsidiary	**a**	Einrichtung
2.	set up	**b**	Kontingent
3.	facility	**c**	Zoll
4.	branch	**d**	gründen
5.	quota	**e**	Filiale
6.	tariff	**f**	Tochtergesellscaft

BRAIN WORK Two: Quiz time

And now a quiz on expanding abroad. Good luck!

1. What is the difference between a subsidiary and a branch?

a A subsidiary is a separate company and a branch is part of the home company

b A subsidiary is part of the home company and a branch is a separate company
c Both words mean the same; a company that has a factory abroad

2. Which of the following sentences from a letter is correct?
a We have retained your address from the Italian Embassy
b We have obtained your address from the Italian Embassy
c We have obtained your adress from the Italian Embassy

3. In which area of business would we expect to hear about quotas and tariffs?
a Production in a factory
b The import and export of goods
c The transport of goods in one country

4. The words 'set up' are used in the correct way in one of the sentences. Which?
a A new factory was set up and a lot workers lost their jobs.
b We wish to set up a factory in France
c I'm sorry but I must set up your answer.

5. When two or more people own the same company they can be called
a The company joints
b The joint owners
c The own jointers

6. If someone said 'you can inspect the site' you would expect to see
a A type of chair
b A place where things can be built or done
c The doctor for an eye test

BRAIN WORK Three: Build up your word power

Use the English words / phrases to translate the German words in the letter.

jobs establish are writing assistance produces due to extend distribution base assemble expanding storage facility offices employees keen on

Dear Mr Crook

We *schreiben* to you as the head of the council in your town as we wish to *gründen* a distribution *Hauptstelle* in your town. We are an American firm, which *herstellt* office furniture in Spain. *Aufgrund* the fact that the market is *expandiert* dramatically in Britain we wish to have *Büros*, a parking area for trucks, *Lagerhalle* and small factory there.
This will result in *Arbeitsplätze* for over sixty people at first but if the business expands there could be over one hundred *Angestellten.*
We have a site in mind on the Hinckley Industrial Park. We are *begeistert von* this site because you are building a new road from it to the A68 road. We will also wish to *vergrößern* the building so that we can *montieren* our office furniture there prior to Verteilung.
Please send us information on any financial *Hilfe* or any other incentives.

Yours faithfully
G Trueman

BRAIN WORK Four: Test your vocabulary!

Here are six sentences in English. Choose the best word form the list to put in the spaces.

loans available sites incentive extend branches set up

1. Mr Crook offered us a large .... to move to Nuneaton.
2. There are many .... for building available in this town.
3. We want to .... the building for storage.
4. Hudson International is a large firm with .... in Southern Europe.
5. Onions wants to .... a production facility in Sydney.
6. Telford makes special .... to companies who bring jobs to the town.

THANKS AND CONGRATULATIONS

Chapter 22

Contents

FOCUS: Maintaining good contacts
DIALOGUE: Good news all round Onions
DROP THEM A LINE: Letters of thanks and congratulations
PUT IT ANOTHER WAY: Alternative phrases
BRAIN WORK: Correct and write a letter

Joke Time

Bob Onion organised a meeting with his sales staff after his visit to China. The time for the meeting was 5 o'clock on Friday afternoon. One of the managers said "Isn't a meeting at this time very inconvenient?[1]"
"Not at all," Onion answered, "it's very convenient for me. You see at that time and at that point[2] in the week nobody wants to argue[3] with me. It's very simple."

1 unbequem 2 Zeit 3 streiten

FOCUS: Maintaining good contacts

Mainly to create goodwill and maintain good business contacts, firms will send letters congratulating good and well-known clients and customers if they get promotion or perhaps even on a more personal level if someone you do business with gets married. There are also times when people in business need to say thank-you, for example, after a visit to a firm where they were looked after in some way by the employees in that company. Although this area is not vital to business, it is important as it creates a good atmosphere and perhaps paves the way for further business.

DIALOGUE: Good news all round at Onions

Bob Onion is meeting members of his sales team, Gerry Murry (**GM**), and Ian Miller (**IM**) after Bob Onion (**BO**) has just come back from a visit to their subsidiary in Shanghai.

IM: So, how was the trip and what's the situation in China?

BO: Wonderful, after we get the bureaucracy sorted out and other paper work it looks like things are looking up!

GM: What about the site and the work force?

BO: Well, we have a small factory on the edge of town. It's really new. We need to install all the machines and pay for telephone lines to the plant. I met some of the managers and the boss of the local firm, Wah Foo Ltd., who are the joint owners of the company. I was very impressed. With the reduced labour costs we can import some of our products back to Europe and make our activities here more competitive.

GM: And won't we need some of our people out there to keep an eye on things?

BO: That is my next point. Thanks to your activities, gentlemen, in developing contacts with the East, this whole deal has come to fruition. Since you, Gerry, have a lot of overseas experience, I have decided to send you over there as the manager. Promotion!

GM: Oh, really!

BO: Yes, a man of your experience will be vital, especially as things on the ground are a little, how should I put it? Yes, er, basic.

GM: Basic?! How basic?

BO: You know, Gerry, we are breaking new ground. I mean the accommodation.

GM: But didn't you say the accommodation was good, I mean you said you lived in the Shanghai Intercontinental, swimming pool, sauna, tennis courts and a three room suite?

BO: I did, but you will need to live close to the plant to keep a good grip on things. The factory is 50 kilometres out of Shanghai and transport being such a problem, well, you need to be there.

GM: So what's wrong with the accommodation there? Local three star hotel?

BO: The problem is there is no accommodation! But a flat is being built at the moment.

GM: When will it be ready?

BO: Well, you need to be out there next month, April and if all goes well the flat will be ready by July. The boss of Wah Foo Ltd. has provided an emergency solution.

GM: What kind of solution?

BO: A hut. It's a comfortable hut, I saw it myself. Oh and Ian, I want you to be head of sales with special responsibility for the Far East here at our plant in the UK.

IM: Thanks a lot, Mr Onion. I'm looking forward to working with Gerry on an international level.

BO: Okay, gentlemen, now that I've given you the good news I need to write a letter of thanks to Wah Foo for taking such good care of me while I was there.

Drop Them A LINE: Letters of thanks and congratulations

Bob Onion, who knows all about good business, wrote a letter of thanks to the boss of the Chinese company, Mr Foo. Here it is.

Dear Mr Foo

Now that I am back in Britain I would like to take the opportunity of thanking you most warmly for the excellent hospitality you extended to me. It was indeed wonderful to have this possibility of meeting you and visiting your company and Shanghai prior to us starting in business together.
I am convinced that our co-operation will be long lasting and successful. I hope and look forward to being able to receiving a visit from you here in Britain in the near future.

I thank you once again, and I am

Sincerely yours,
Robert Onion

Ian Miller, having been promoted at Onions, was sent a letter from a customer in Germany, Mr Gruber:

Dear Mr Miller

It was with great pleasure that I was informed by Frau Dietz, our UK buyer, that you have been promoted to head of sales for the Far East. May I take the opportunity of congratulating you most sincerely on this promotion and wish you every success in the future?
With my personal regards

Yours sincerely
Fritz Gruber

VOCABULARY: To help you understand

accommodation	*Unterkunft*
all round	*ringsum*
basic	*einfach, elementar*
break new ground	*Neuland erschließen*
bureaucracy	*Bürokratie*
congratulation	*Glückwunsch*
convinced	*überzeugt*
create	*erzeugen*
edge	*Rand*
emergency solution	*Notlösung*
employee	*Arbeitnehmer*
excellent	*ausgezeichnet*
extend hospitality	*Gastfreundschaft erweisen*
flat	*Wohnung*
fruition; bring to ~	*aufblühen lassen*
goodwill	*Wohlwollen*
hospitality	*Gastfreundlichkeit*
hut	*Hütte*
impressed	*beeindruckt*
keep a good grip on	*im Griff haben*
keep an eye on	*die Sache im Auge behalten*
long lasting	*lange während*
look after	*sich kümmern um*
look up (things are looking up)	*es geht bergauf*
mainly	*hauptsächlich*
maintain	*aufrechterhalten*
pave the way	*den Weg ebnen*
pleasure	*Freude*
prior	*bevor*
promotion	*Beförderung*
sort out	*erledigen*
take the opportunity	*die Gelegenheit ergreifen*
virtually	*fast*

vital	*sehr wichtig*
warmly	*herzlich*
work force	*Arbeitskraft*

Put it ANOTHER WAY: Alternative phrases

Saying thank you	
this is just to thank you once again	hiermit möchte ich Ihnen nochmals danken
I want to thank you most sincerely	ich möchte Ihnen aufrichtig danken
I feel that this meeting was most beneficial to future business	ich denke, dass dieses Treffen für unsere zukünftigen Geschäfte sehr förderlich war
thank you very much for an excellent meal	ich danke Ihnen für eine ausgezeichnete Mahlzeit
I hope you will give me the opportunity of reciprocating before long	ich hoffe, dass Sie mir die Gelegenheit geben, mich bald erkenntlich zu zeigen

Congratulations	
I am writing to convey my warm congratulations	ich möchte Ihnen herzlich gratulieren
this is a brief note to say "congratulations"	ich möchte Ihnen kurz gratulieren
I was pleased to learn of your promotion	ich habe mich gefreut, von Ihrer Beförderung zu erfahren

BRAIN WORK One: Correct the letter

Please take a look at this letter and find the mistakes made by someone in the office. Use Bob Onion's letter to help you. Oh yes, there are nine mistakes.

Dear Mr Peabody

This is to thank you mostly sincere and warmly for the excellent hospital you extended me.
It was indeed wonderful to have this possibility of to meeting you and your managers.
I hop and look forward to be able to receiving a visitor from you here in England.

Yours sincerely
Fred Dolittle

BRAIN WORK Two: Put in the words

Over to you to put in the following words in the sentences below. Use the words and phrases in this chapter to help you.

reciprocating extending promotion take sincerely pleasure

1. Thank you for ... your hospitality to me during my visit.
2. I want to thank you most ... for an excellent meal.
3. We were very pleased to learn of your ...
4. I now wish to ... the opportunity of thanking you.
5. It was with great ... that I learned of your promotion.
6. I hope that you will give me the opportunity of ... before long.

BRAIN WORK Three: Writing a letter

Here are some sentences from a letter written by the representative of a firm thanking a manager for a visit. The sentences are all mixed up and need putting in order to create a good letter.

I hope that you will give us the chance of inviting you to see us in Belgrade.
Once again many thanks.
I feel that this meeting will be very beneficial for future business contacts.
I am writing this letter to say that I was most pleased to have the opportunity of meeting you at your factory in Wolverhampton.

BRAIN WORK Four: Build up your vocabulary

Put the English word / phrase with the correct German word / phrase.

1.	once again	**a**	aufblühen lassen
2.	take the opportunity	**b**	Gastfreundschaft beweisen
3.	extend hospitality	**c**	die Gelegenheit ergreifen
4.	promotion	**d**	nochmals
5.	pave the way	**e**	den Weg ebnen
6.	things are looking up	**f**	Beförderung
7.	bring the fruition	**g**	sich kümmern um
8.	look after	**h**	es geht bergauf

USING EMAILS

Chapter 23

Contents

FOCUS: Emailing
DIALOGUE: Bob Onions and emails
DROP THEM A LINE: Good email style
PUT IT ANOTHER WAY: Alternative phrases
BRAIN WORK: Test your email style

Joke Time

One morning a technician in the computer support department gets a telephone call.

Technician: Hello, help desk here.
Manager: Hello, can you help me? My computer won't work.
Technician: Really. Have you turned it on[1]?
Manager: Yes I've turned it on.
Technician: Is there a little light on[2] at the front?
Manager: No, no little light.
Technician: Is the computer plugged in[3] with the switches on?
Manager: Yes.
Technician: Ok now look at the back of the computer. Is the cable plugged in?
Manager: Actually it's hard to say, I can't see very well, it's very dark.
Technician: What do you mean? Dark?
Manager: You see the lights are out because of the power cut[4].

1 einschalten 2 brennt ein kleines Licht 3 angeschlossen 4 Stromausfall

FOCUS: Emailing

The email has become very important both inside an organisation and outside. The email can be used to send short notes organising lunch with a colleague in the next office, arranging a meeting overseas or sending the plans of a diesel motor by attachment for example. The advantage of an email is that it is quick and reliable. You can send an email to a whole department or to a group of ten people in ten different countries. Imagine writing the letters, putting them in envelopes and taking them to the post office for the different stamps.

Writing letters has its own style and the same is true for emails. Remember the reason for sending emails is that we want to be clear and pass on our message quickly but also politely. Writing clearly then has a number of good points:

- It saves you and your reader time – the reader does not need to work hard to understand your message.
- It reduces confusion.
- It will make your reader think you have a good business manner.

It is also a good idea to ask for an immediate reply so that you know your email has been received especially on first contact or when the business is very important. This can be done by using asking for an email back or a phone call or by using the 'receipt acknowledgement facility' normally found on email systems.

DIALOGUE: Bob Onions and emails

Bob Onions (**BO**) is talking to Mick Miles (**MM**) the IT manager.

BO: I don't know but things have changed, Mick. Maybe I'm too old for this game. I just get used to computers then it's something else, cell phones, email. Isn't writing a letter more important than writing emails. I get dozens of emails a day and spend an hour answering them. And the style. It all seems too informal to me.

MM: The fact is that answering an email isn't an obligation, it's an opportunity. You can use replies as a springboard for doing more business, encourage future sales. If you reply quickly it makes a good impression. Even if an email is to register a complaint it helps foster good business relationships. Statistics show that between 70 and 90 percent of complainants will do business with you if a complaint is sorted out quickly and satisfactorily.

BO: You and your statistics. Can't we have a standard email and get the computer to do it for us?

MM: Well we can save time by having a standard response. We should analyse what type of emails we get over a week and put them into areas like complaints, requests for information, customer suggestions and then analyse them in more detail. In complaints there will be problems with quality, service, price, availability and so on. Then we can create standard replies.

BO: Well I am still in the dark. I could go with a few tips.

MM: Write emails like you speak: not too formally. Write like a conversation and your words should show some personality to help develop contact. Don't forget KISS.

BO: What, put kisses at the end?

MM: No! Keep It Simple Stupid! Make your sentences short and to the point. Be less formal but don't go over the top! Don't sound over friendly!

BO: Well no danger there!

Drop Them A LINE: Good email style

It is important that the customers feel that you think about them. This email is in answer to a small complaint.

Dear Susan Nelson

Thanks for your email. We are always keen to learn the comments and views of our customers – it's a very important way for us to improve and develop both service and products. So we're grateful you went out of your way to contact us and we'll definitely take what you say into account.

Thanks once again
Kind regards
Debby Harris

Look at the email to a customer.

Dear Paul

Many thanks for your email. For info about our pumps please visit our web site – www.Onions.com.
Just go to the 'Information on Products' box at the top left and click on 'Electronic Motors'.
You should find all the answers to your queries there. If not then please don't hesitate to email. Also if you have any other questions about our products simply get in touch.
Kind regards
Mick

Note: It is also a good idea to write a date with your email if a deadline is important.

Smileys or Emoticons

Be careful about the use of smileys in business contexts. Here are some examples:

: -)	THE USER IS HAPPY.
8 -)	THE USER IS WEARING GLASSES.
; -)	THE USER IS IRONIC.
: -(	THE USER IS UNHAPPY.
:- O	THE USER SAYS „OH NO!“
: - /	THE USER IS SCEPTICAL.

You should remember that not everybody understands them and what you think is funny may not be funny to somebody else. Also the emoticons may be seen as unprofessional and are not appropriate in a business context.

Abbreviations and symbols

All abbreviations and symbols are really to reduce time spent keying in letters. Remember that some people may see this as lazy or even sloppy. Good commercial emails require the writer to walk a fine line between friendly and informative on one hand and over informal and irrelevant on the other.

On the subject of symbols is a technical point that the person receiving your email may not have the same software or so-called text editor. Underlining __can be a problem as can the asterisk *. The (TM) symbol meaning trademark can also be problematic. With £ & $ ¥ „ for example it is often better to write them out in full. You may think you have sent a certain symbol but the recipient gets something else. This is not good for communication.

Some people like to use abbreviations like 'cu' pronounced as the letters 'see you' or 'bfn' meaning 'bye for now'.

Last of all here your motto should be: if you have a doubt leave it out!

Don'ts in writing business emails
Don't use slang.
Don't be boring.
Don't swear.
Don't get angry.
Don't use computer jargon like emoticons.
Don't use formal long sentences.
Don't use passive verbs.

VOCABULARY: To help you understand

abbreviation	*Abkürzung*
account; take into ~	*in Betracht ziehen*
advantage	*Vorteil*
analyse	*analysieren*
and so on	*und so weiter*
area	*Gebiet*
cell phone	*Handy*
context	*Zusammenhang*
create	*erzeugen*
dark; I'm in the ~	*keine Ahnung haben*
definitely	*bestimmt*
encourage	*ermutigen, anregen*

foster	*fördern*
impression; make a good ~	*einen guten Eindruck machen*
irrelevant	*nebensächlich*
key in	*eintippen*
overseas	*Übersee*
reliable	*zuverlässig*
sloppy	*schlampig*
sort out	*in Ordnung bringen*
springboard	*Sprungbrett*
stamp	*Briefmarke*

Put It ANOTHER WAY: Alternative phrases

Starting an email

You should always err on the side of caution[1]. You can start emails:

Dear David Beckham, or
Dear Mr Beckham or
Dear David or
Hi Dave

This depends on your feelings and how well you know the person. Do not start emails 'Dear Sir / Madam' as this is too formal. You could even start with 'Hi' if you feel it's ok to do so.

Ending an email

'Yours Sincerely' etc is much too formal. Here are some alternatives:

Regards
Kind / kindest regards
Best regards / wishes
All the best
Wishing you well
Cheers

1 Man sollte im Zweifelsfall lieber zu vorsichtig sein

'Regards' sounds a little cold. 'Wishing you well' is fine but perhaps not right for business. 'Kind regards / best regards' sounds friendly but not too informal. Do not be surprised to hear and see 'cheers'.
In modern British English 'cheers' now is not only said when having a drink (in fact not said that often in this situation) but is often used to mean 'thanks' and 'bye'. This is very informal and should not be used in business emails unless you know the person getting the email. British people will be impressed to hear you use it correctly though.

Language in emails

Generally be less formal in emails so that the language is more like spoken English. Here are some examples:

We appreciated / were grateful for	Thanks for	Wir waren dankbar für
We refer to	About	Wir beziehen uns auf
As requested	As you asked	Wunschgemäß
Please forward us	Please send us	Bitte senden Sie uns
Please advise us	Please tell us	Bitte teilen Sie uns mit
We regret that	We're sorry that	Wir bedauern, dass
If the time does not suit you	If the time isn't OK by you	Falls die Zeit Ihnen nicht passt
We are forced to inform you	We have got to tell you	Wir müssen Ihnen mitteilen

BRAIN WORK One: A quiz on using emails

1. Two wrong answers three correct answers. You decide which.
You should not use Smileys in business emails because:
a Some people in offices do not understand what all Smileys mean.
b Some people think that Smileys are not appropriate in a business context.
c Managers do not want people to be happy in the office and Smileys are fun.
d You may think something is funny but the recipient may not.
e Smileys make people sloppy and lazy.

2. Which of the following sentences is true?
a Emails should be as formal as normal business letters.
b You should use passive sentences as much as possible with emails.
c You should be careful about using symbols and abbreviations.

3. Here are some possible ways of ending an email and some impossible ways. Decide which are possible and decide which are most and least formal.
a Best regards
b All the best
c Yours respectfully
d Cheers
e Sincerely yours
f bfn
g Bottoms up

4. You should answer emails to customers promptly because
a it gives you something to do.
b it makes the boss think you are a computer expert.
c it fosters good business relations.

BRAIN WORK Two: Can you change your style of writing?

Convert these sentences from formal letters into email type sentences.

1. We are very grateful for the information you forwarded to us.
2. We are forced to inform you that the goods were lost in transit.
3. If you should have any questions regarding our products do not hesitate to contact us.
4. We are indeed very sorry to inform you that...
5. We would be grateful if you could let us know by phone when you will visit us.

BRAIN WORK Three: A little grammar exercise

You should avoid long passive sentences when writing emails. Change these sentences into good email style.

1. The goods have been damaged by sand.
2. You will be visited by our manager, Mrs Oldfield, in May.
3. The pumps will be packed in wooden crates by our despatch department.
4. Upon opening the boxes it was found that a mistake had been made.
5. The letter was posted last Friday
6. It is to be regretted that I cannot attend the meeting.
7. The problem is being discussed at the meeting on Friday.
8. A discount of 25 percent will be granted for orders in excess of 500.

TOP 30 MISTAKES QUIZ

Now we can check up on what you have learned so far. Decide which word is best in each sentence.

1. Yours faithfully / Yours sincerely
If a letter begins Dear Madam it should end with ___________?

2. appreciate / like
a We would __________ it very much if you could send us a brochure.
b Customers do not ___________ waiting more than a few minutes.

3. for / since
a We have been selling insurance __________ twenty years.
b The company has been exporting _________ 1958.

4. receive / receiving
a We are looking forward to _____________ an order from you.
b When can we __________ the goods?

5. by / until
a The goods must be sent ____________ Tuesday at the latest.
b I will stay in Huddersfield _________ 2nd April then fly back to Ankara.

6. control / check
a Please _________ that you have sent the crates to the correct address.
b There will be problems for our firm if the government does not _________ imports.

7. note / notice
a Please _________ that we will be on holiday the second week of July.
b There was a _____________ on the door '12.30 until 13.45 Lunch'.

8. to / without
a I refer _________ you enquiry dated 12th May.
b This offer is ___________ engagement.

9. while / until

a We can supply you __________ stocks last.

b We can supply you __________ stocks have all be sold.

10. for / of

a We wish to thank you ________ you interest.

b You may rely on the prompt execution _______ your order.

11. prompt / soon

a We thank you for your _______ response to our complaint.

b The goods will arrive very __________ the manager said.

12. from / on

a The cost of coffee depends _______ the weather in Brazil.

b We ordered 20 bags of Arabica coffee _______ Allison & Sons.

13. overlooked / looked over

a We are very sorry but it seems we __________ the bill. You will receive payment tomorrow.

b The customer __________ the goods before they were packed to check on their condition.

14. let / leave

a Please ________ us have you order in the next two weeks.

b I will _________ for Spain next Monday.

15. out / in

a We will send the products ________ the following two days.

b We must point ______ that your account has not been cleared.

16. overdue / due

a Payment is _______ on the first day of each month.

b Payment is now three weeks ____________.

17. on / in

a We are very keen _________ importing your products

b I am interested _________ visiting your factory.

18. in / at

a The factory is normally closed ________ the weekends.

b We want to order the products ______ June.

19. grant / make

a We will __________ a discount for large orders.

b They wished to _________ a complaint.

20. made / placed

a The company __________ a large order.

b We will __________ you an offer soon.

21. by / in

a She has worked __________ the purchasing department for ten years.

b The toilets are in the corridor _________ the lifts.

22. could you please send / send

a I've told you twice, __________ the documents to the bank!

b We do not wish to create any inconvenience but _____________ the document to our bank?

23. in / on

a The goods were despatched __________ 12th July.

b We will be in England _________ July.

24. fabric / factory

a The overalls are made from a nylon __________ in five different colours.

b The _________ in Argentina is the newest in South America.

25. on / without

a We noted that the goods were in good order ________ checking them.

b We cannot receive payment __________ sending the documents to their bank.

26. direction / management

a If you want to find the sales manager go in this _________ then turn left.

b The _______________ hope that you enjoyed your visit.

27. had / made

a They have ________ a lot of experience selling in the Middle East.

b We also ___________ many business contacts last year at the trade fair.

28. prospects / brochures
a There are positive __________ for the sale of helicopters to Spain.
b I am sorry but we do not have any ____________ in this department.

29. most up-to-date / actual
a The _________ reason for the delay was because of the manager.
b Please send us your _____________ price list and conditions.

30. information / details
a Enclosed is some ___________ about our product line.
b Please note these ___________ as you will need them to obtain payment.

KEY

1.	Yours faithfully		**16.**	**a** due	**b** overdue
2.	**a** appreciate	**b** like	**17.**	**a** on	**b** in
3.	**a** for	**b** since	**18.**	**a** at	**b** in
4.	**a** receiving	**b** receive	**19.**	**a** grant	**b** make
5.	**a** by	**b** until	**20.**	**a** placed	**b** made
6.	**a** check	**b** control	**21.**	**a** in	**b** by
7.	**a** note	**b** notice	**22.**	**a** send	**b** could you please send
8.	**a** to	**b** without	**23.**	**a** on	**b** in
9.	**a** while	**b** until	**24.**	**a** fabric	**b** factory
10.	**a** for	**b** of	**25.**	**a** on	**b** without
11.	**a** prompt	**b** soon	**26.**	**a** direction	**b** management
12.	**a** on	**b** from	**27.**	**a** had	**b** made
13.	**a** overlooked	**b** looked over	**28.**	**a** prospects	**b** brochures
14.	**a** let	**b** leave	**29.**	**a** actual	**b** most up-to-date
15.	**a** in	**b** out	**30.**	**a** information	**b** details

CLASSROOM ACTIVITIES

Enquiries

For this activity the class can work in pairs or two groups.
One group or person writes an enquiry to Allison Ltd, a company that produces photographic equipment. You are interested in selling enlargers (Vergrößerer) and other photography equipment for your business. The name of your firm is 'Cameras Are Us'. You have the name of the Allison Ltd from a trade journal and the Internet. Ask for a current price list, delivery times and conditions. Say that you will place large / regular orders if the quality is up to expectations and prices are competitive.

The other group or person writes an enquiry to 'Fredrick Sporting Goods'. Start by saying that you visited their stand at the Frankfurt Trade Fair earlier this year. You are the buyer for a large chain of sports shops in Germany called 'Sport World'. You are very interested in footballs, which you noted are very competitively priced. Say that you want an up-to-date catalogue with full price list. Also say that you may be interested in other equipment but that depends on conditions and prices.

Offers

The first group / person now changes roles. You are to write a reply (offer) from 'Fredrick Sporting Goods' to 'Sport World'. In your offer you need to include the following information:

1. Say thanks for the enquiry.
2. Say that an up-to-date catalogue and price list is included.
3. Say that each football the price is $12.75 for 10 footballs the price is $105.50 and more than 10 you grant a discount of 20 percent. Prices are quoted CIF and a further discount (7 percent) is granted if payment is made within a week..
4. Say that you can supply golf, tennis and rugby balls at competitive prices.
5. Say that your offer is valid for a month and hope to hear from them soon.

The second group / person changes roles. You write a reply (offer) from 'Allison Ltd' to 'Cameras Are Us'. The following information is to be included:

1. Say thanks for their interest.
2. Say a current price list, delivery times and conditions is included.
3. Say you can supply a number of enlargers but see enclosed catalogue.
4. Recommend the Z104 priced at $650. You can supply a limited number (55 left in stock) as this type will not be in production after this month the price is very low. The latest model that replaces the Z104, the Z108, will cost $895. See list of conditions for discounts.
5. Say that the offer is valid for two weeks but Z104 is very popular. You look forward to getting an order.

Queries and Offers

Each person or small group should write queries based on real information of a product they know. The another group / person should then read the query and write an offer.

Orders and Acknowledgements / Confirmations

The class can form into groups of two people. Each group will write an order based on the following short notes (the product you want to order is your choice).

1. Refer to quotation of any date.
2. Say that you want to order X number of Y products.
3. Delivery will be within one month of receipt of order.
4. State price ex works including packaging.
   Now pass round the letters. Read them and write a short acknowledgement / confirmation of each one.

Cancellation

As a group how many ways can you think of to say that you are sorry? Next think of as many reasons as you can why an order might be cancelled. Write short letters in small groups or individuals cancelling the following giving a good reason why.

1. A two week holiday in Mallorca.
2. A special order for 20 bicycles for three people (with three saddles).
3. A conference room booked for five days (booked six months ago).
4. An order for 300 monitors.
5. Five hundred kilos of tomatoes (ripe).
   Discuss the letters.

Replies to Cancellations

Write letters back to the cancellations in which you say you understand the problem but explain that you will now lose money / have no use for the products (give reasons why) and that you want compensation.

Delays

As a group think of as many reasons why you cannot supply a product. Write a letter in pairs / small groups explaining why you cannot deliver on time the following products:

1. A shipment of 400 20 kilo bags of coffee beans from Brazil.
2. An order for thirty woollen pullovers from Galway in Ireland.
3. A delivery of 2000 turbo chargers for cars from Birmingham in England.
4. Two crates of top quality porcelain from Toulouse.
5. Thirty 20 bottle crates of British beer and 100 kilos of Stilton cheese.
   Pass round the letters and write a reply.

Payment

First in teams or small groups think of ways of giving a good reason / excuse why you could not pay on time. Now write a letter explaining a delay in payment. Now think of as many ways you can of telling people that they need to pay your bill. Pass on the first letter to another group and write a letter asking for payment. The next step is to repeat the activity until somebody says that they will contact a lawyer.

Arranging Meetings

Discuss why we need meetings and where these meetings can take place. In groups write letters to other groups requesting a meeting arranging a time and place. Pass on the letters and reply to the letters first confirming them and then sending a further letter/fax/email saying that there is a problem (think of a problem) on that day and postponing the meeting.

Complaints

As a group discuss how you can complain about something thinking about alternative ways of complaining in a letter. In groups/pairs take one problem from the list and write a complaint. Look at each other's letters and then decide what type of letter you could write back.

1. You ordered 500 black biros (Kugelschreiber) but 5000 blue biros arrived.
2. You are unhappy about the conference centre and hotel rooms you booked for your staff.
3. You ordered 10 crates of jars of marmalade. Three crates were damaged and the marmalade spoilt.
4. The 50 squash rackets you ordered and received seem to have been damaged by water.
5. You received the wrong model vacuum cleaner (Staubsauger).
6. You arranged a holiday but at least three things went wrong.

Applying for a Job

In whole group think about different jobs (you could bring in jobs advertised in newspapers). Suggest ways of writing a letter as a group. Then think about a number of jobs in your organisation and what each job requires. In small groups write letters of application and pass round the letters. Which letter would get a positive response and why?

Fairs and Exhibitions

In small groups or pairs write out details of an exhibition (give the exhibition a good name, give dates, costs for exhibitors, place etc). Now in small groups decide that you wish to exhibit a product. Write a letter to another group who answers you as the exhibition organisers. Write further letters one in confirmation and then another letter asking to alter the conditions for your exhibition.

Banking

Imagine in groups or as individuals that you are a bank manager writing to another member of the class. Write a letter asking the recipient to do something about their financial problems. After the letter is passed to the other student a write a reply giving a really good excuse.

Subsidiaries

In groups or as individuals imagine that your company produces as product that you want to produce overseas. Decide where you wish to produce the goods and why. Write a letter to a possible company talking about your business. Enquire about the firm and suggest production of your goods. Pass the letter to someone else in the group. The other person writes a reply. Read out the letters.

Emails

Write emails to other group members. The subjects are:

1. Arrange a drink after work.
2. Apologise for not being at a meeting.
3. Ask about a delay in delivery of a product.
4. Ask if the recipient wants to meet for dinner.
5. Enquire about holidays in Peru.
6. Arrange a meeting.
7. Say sorry that a mistake has been made with a delivery.
8. Complain about your car to a garage.
9. Tell the recipient that you will visit their firm next week.
10. On a holiday the water in the hotel was cut off so complain to the holiday company.

After you have written emails pass them to the other group members. Write a reply.

LETTER FUNCTIONS

Die englische Sprache ist sehr reich an Ausdrücken gleicher oder ähnlicher Bedeutung. Deshalb finden Sie in diesem systematischen Überblick für einen deutschen Satz oft mehrere englische Sätze. Außerdem ist es nicht immer möglich, eine deutsche Entsprechung für alle englischen Redemittel zu finden.

Briefe beginnen

Besten Dank für Ihren Brief vom ... mit der Anfrage über ...

Many thanks for your letter dated ... with the enquiry about ...
or
Thanks a lot for your letter of ... enquiring about ...

Vielen Dank für Ihren Brief vom ... mit der Mitteilung, dass ...

Thank you for your letter dated ... advising us that ... / informing us that ... / with the information that ... / telling us that ...

Wir danken Ihnen für Ihren Brief vom ... mit der beigefügten Preisliste

We thank you for your letter of ... with the enclosed price list / enclosing your price list

Besten Dank für Ihre heutige E-Mail.	Thanks for today's email.
Ihre E-Mail hat uns sehr gefreut.	We are very pleased to receive / get your email.
Wir schreiben an Sie, um ...	We are writing to you to ...
Es tut mir Leid, Sie davon zu informieren, dass ...	I regret to inform you that ...
Wir bedauern sehr, Ihrem Schreiben vom ... zu entnehmen, dass ...	We are extremely sorry to learn from your letter dated ... that ...
Es freut uns zu hören, dass ...	We are pleased to hear that ... **or** We are happy to hear that ... **or** We are glad to hear that ...
Wir entnehmen Ihrem Brief vom ..., dass ...	We note from your letter dated ... that ...
Im Anschluß an meinen Brief vom ... sende ich Ihnen ...	Further to my letter of ... I am sending you ...
Mit Bezug auf unseren vorhergehenden Brief möchten wir darauf hinweisen, dass ...	Refering to our previous letter, we wish to point out that... **or** With reference to our previous correspondance, we should like to point out that ...
Wie ich in meinem vorigen Brief erwähnt habe ...	As I mentioned in my previous letter ...
In unserem letzten Brief vom ... haben wir erklärt, dass ...	In our last letter, dated ..., we explained that ...
Im Anschluss an unser Telefongespräch ...	Further to our telephone call ...
Ich beziehe mich auf den Bericht ...	I refer to the report ...
Wir schreiben jetzt, um zu bestätigen, dass ...	We are now writing to conform that ...

Bitte nehmen Sie in der E-Mail zur Kenntnis, dass ...	Please note in the email that ...
Hiermit möchte ich bestätigen, dass ...	I wish to confirm that ...

Briefe beenden

Wir hoffen, in der nahen Zukunft/ in Kürze/bald/so bald wie möglich von Ihnen zu hören.	We look forward to hearing from you in the near future/shortly/soon/as soon as possible.
Ich hoffe, bald von Ihnen zu hören.	We hope to hear from you shortly
Wir wären sehr dankbar, von Ihnen so bald wie möglich zu hören.	We would be extremely grateful to hear from you as soon as possible. **or** We would be very thankful if you contacted us as soon as possible.
Ich würde eine sofortige Antwort sehr schätzen.	A prompt reply would be much/ greatly appreciated. **or** I would/should appreciate a prompt reply.
Dürfen wir bald von Ihnen hören?	May we hear from you soon? **or** We trust we will hear from you shortly.
Können Sie uns bitte durch E-Mail/Fax mitteilen ...	Could you please inform us by email/fax ...
Da diese Sache äußerst eilig ist, antworten Sie uns bitte innerhalb der nächsten Tage.	As this matter is very/extremely urgent please/kindly let us have a reply/an answer within the next few days. **or** Since this is a matter of great/extreme urgency would you please reply/ answer within the next few days.
Bitte behandeln Sie diese Sache als äußerst dringend.	Please treat this matter with the greatest urgency/utmost urgency.
Wir erwarten eine Antwort bis nächsten Montag.	We expect a response by Monday next.

Antworten Sie uns bitte unbedingt bis nächsten Dienstag.	Kindly let us have your reply by next Tuesday without fail.
Wir wären für eine Antwort möglichst/ spätestens bis zum ... dankbar.	We would appreciate an answer by ... if possible/at the latest.
Wir hoffen, dass die Sendung in gutem Zustand bei Ihnen ankommt.	We trust/hope that the consignment will arrive in good condition.
Mit vielem Dank im Voraus.	Thanking you in advance.

Anfragen

Bitte nennen Sie uns Ihre Preise für...	Please quote your prices for ...
Bitte schicken Sie uns Ihre äußersten Preise für ...	Please quote your best/keenest/ lowest prices for ...
Bitte schicken Sie uns weitere Einzelheiten über ...	Please let us have further information about/concerning ...
Können Sie ab Lager liefern?	Can you supply from stock?
Können Sie uns sofort ... liefern?	Are you able to supply us with ... straight away? **or** Can you deliver ... immediately? **or** Are you in a position to let us have ... without delay?
Machen Sie uns bitte ein Angebot über ... und nennen Sie den frühesten Liefertermin.	Please let us have a quotation for ... and the earliest date of delivery. **or** Would you please quote for ... stating/giving the earliest delivery date.
Sie wurden uns von ... empfohlen.	You have been recommended to us by ...
Ihre Firma wurde uns empfohlen.	Your firm has been recommended to us.
Wir haben von Ihrer Firma durch das Internet erfahren.	We have heard of your firm via the Internet.
Vorausgesetzt, dass Ihre Preise angemessen/günstig sind, ...	Provided that your prices are reasonable/favourable ...

Wenn Ihre Preisangabe konkurrenzfähig ist, wären wir zu einem großen Auftrag / Probeauftrag bereit.	If your quotation is competitive, we would be prepared to place a substantial / trial order.
Wir beabsichtigen einen Auftrag zu erteilen, falls die Qualität der Waren unseren Erwartungen entspricht.	We intend to place an order if the quality of the goods meets / comes up to our expectations / requirements.
Wir wären für Auskünfte über ... dankbar.	We would be grateful for information regarding / about ...
Wir benötigen ...	We require / need ... **or** We have a requirement for ... **or** We have a need for ...
Wir haben von ... erfahren, dass Sie ... herstellen.	We have heard from ... that you produce ...
Wir sind daran interessiert, ... zu importieren.	We are interested in importing ...
Wir wären sehr dankbar für die Zusendung Ihres neuesten Katalogs und ausführlicher Informationen über ...	We should / would be very grateful if you could send / forward us your latest catalogue and detailed information about ...
Wir werden einen großen Auftrag erteilen, wenn die Qualität der Waren zufriedenstellend ist.	We will place a large order if the quality of the goods is satisfactory.
Wir würden gerne Ihre neueste Preisliste und Exportbedingungen erhalten.	We would / should be glad / pleased to recieve your most up to date / latest / current price list and export conditions.

Angebote

ab Werk	ex works
frei an Bord	FOB (Free On Board)
Kosten Versicherung Fracht	CIF (Cost Insurance Freight)
frachtfrei	carriage paid

Bitte beachten Sie, dass alle Preise einem Rabatt von ... Prozent unterliegen	Please note that all prices are subject to a discount of ... per cent.
Beiliegend senden wir Ihnen vollständige Angaben über Preise, Mengen, Verkaufsbedingungen sowie über Liefertermine.	Enclosed you will find full information / details about / concerning prices, quantities, conditions / terms of sale as well as delivery dates.
Unsere Preise schließen Verpackung und Transport ein.	Our prices include packing and carriage.
Unsere Preise verstehen sich FOB ...	Our prices are quoted FOB ...
Wir entnehmen sehr gerne Ihrem Schreiben, dass Sie sich für unsere Geräte interessieren.	We are pleased to learn from your letter that you are interested in our devices.
Wir gewähren einen Rabatt von ... Prozent	We grant a discount of ... per cent
Wir haben uns über Ihre E-Mail / Ihr Fax sehr gefreut.	We were most pleased to get your email / fax.
Wir haben uns sehr über Ihre Anfrage von ... gefreut.	We were very pleased to receive your offer of ... **or** It was with great / considerable pleasure that we received your offer of ... **or** We were extremely glad to receive your offer dated ...
Wunschgemäß senden wir Ihnen gerne den Katalog mit Einzelheiten über ...	We are sending you, as requested / desired our catalogue containing details about ...
Dieses Angebot ist unverbindlich.	This offer is without engagement.
Dieses Angebot ist gültig / fest für ...	This offer is firm / valid for ...
Wir versichern Ihnen, dass Ihr Auftrag zu Ihrer vollen Zufriedenheit ausgeführt wird.	We assure / wish to assure you that **or** You may rest assured that your order will be executed / performed / carried out to your entire satisfaction.

Sie können sich auf die sorgfältige Ausführung Ihres Auftrags verlassen.	You can / may rely on the careful execution / performance of you order.
Wir freuen uns darauf, mit Ihnen ins Geschäft zu kommen.	We look forward to doing business with you.

Aufträge

Wir sind mit den Bedingungen einverstanden.	We agree to the conditions / terms.
Wir müssen darauf aufmerksam machen, dass ...	We must point out that ...
Ich muss Sie daran erinnern, dass ...	I must remind you that ...
Der uns von Frau Hudson angegebene Preis war ...	The price quoted by Mrs Hudson was ...
Bitte bestätigen Sie den Erhalt dieses Auftrags.	Please acknowledge this order.
Bitte liefern Sie uns die nachstehend einzeln aufgeführten Waren.	Please supply us with **or** Please let us have **or** Kindly send us the goods specified below.
Bitte stornieren Sie den Auftrag.	Please cancel the order.
Die Qualität der Waren muss mit der der gelieferten Muster übereinstimmen.	The quality of the goods must correspond to / be in accordance with that of the samples submitted / supplied.
Ich hoffe, dass Sie diesen Auftrag pünktlich erledigen werden.	I hope / trust you will execute this order in good time.
Bitte liefern Sie die Waren sofort.	Please supply the goods immediately.
Bitte sorgen Sie für sofortige Lieferung.	Please arrange for immediate delivery.
Der Auftrag ist besonders dringend.	The order is particularly urgent.
Wir erwarten die erste Sendung innerhalb von 14 Tagen.	We expect the first delivery within 14 days.

Liefern Sie mir bitte die folgenden Artikel postwendend.	Please supply me with the following goods by return.
Wir bedauern, unseren Auftrag Nummer ... stornieren zu müssen.	We regret having to cancel order number ... **or** We are sorry being forced/compelled to cancel our order number ... **or** We regret that we must cancel order number ...
Wir danken Ihnen für Ihr Angebot von ... und bitten Sie um die Lieferung von ...	We thank you for your offer dated ... and would be pleased if you would supply ...
Wir hoffen, dass diese nur die erste von vielen Bestellungen sein wird.	We trust/hope that this will be the first of many orders.
Wir möchten Sie daran erinnern, dass unsere Kunden um sofortige Lieferung gebeten haben.	We would/should like to remind you that our custmers requested immediate delivery.
Wir müssen darauf aufmerksam machen, dass sorgfältige Verpackung unbedingt erforderlich ist.	We must point out that careful packing is essential. **or** We must draw your attention to the fact that the careful packing of the goods is of great importance.
Wir sind, wenn auch ungern, gezwungen, die Bestellung zu stornieren.	It is with great reluctance that we are compelled to cancel the order. **or** We are reluctanty forced to cancel the order.

Auftragsbestätigungen

Die Waren werden in wenigen Tagen abgesandt werden.	The goods will be sent/despatched within a few days.
Vielen Dank für Ihren Auftrag.	Many thanks for your order.

Wir bedauern, dass wir nicht in der Lage sind, die von Ihnen bestellten Waren zu liefern.	We regret that we cannot supply / deliver the goods you ordered.
Wir danken Ihnen für Ihre Bestellung, erteilt am ...	We thank you for your order placed on ...
Wir hoffen, dass dies der erste von vielen Aufträgen sein wird.	We hope / trust that this will be the first of many orders.
Wir sind sicher, dass Sie voll zufrieden mit der Ausführung Ihres Auftrags sein werden.	We are / feel confident / sure / certain that you will be absolutely / completely / fully satisfied with the execution of your order.
Wir werden uns sehr bemühen, die Fertigung Ihres Auftrags rechtzeitig zu erfüllen.	We will do our best / utmost to complete the order in good time.
Leider führen wir diesen Artikel nicht mehr.	Unfortunately we no longer stock this item.
Leider sind wir nicht in der Lage, die bestellten Waren zu liefern.	Unfortunately, we are unable / not in a position to supply the goods you ordered. **or** We regret being unable to supply the goods ordered by you.

Lieferungen und Verzögerungen

Wir können sofort versenden, da alle Waren ab Lager lieferbar sind.	We can deliver at once as / since all goods are available from stock.
Wir können keinen sofortigen Versand garantieren, da viele Waren knapp sind.	We are unable to guarantee immediate delivery / despatch as many goods are in short supply.
Wir möchten Ihnen versichern, dass wir alles tun, um Ihren Auftrag auf den Weg zu bringen.	We wish to assure you that we are doing everything / all in our power to despatch your order.
Die Lieferung kann vor ... erfolgen.	We can effect delivery before ...

Wir sind in der Lage, die Lieferung mit unseren Lastwagen / Lieferwagen zu arrangieren.	We are able to / can arrange shipment / delivery by our truck / van.
Wir können die Sendung per Bahn innerhalb von ... nach Auftragserteilung liefern.	We could send / ship the consignment by rail within ... of receiving your order. **or** It would be possible for us to forward the shipment within four days of receipt of your order.
Wir freuen uns, Ihnen mitteilen zu können, dass die ... heute mit der Bahn versandt wurden.	We are pleased / happy to inform / advise you that the ... have been despatched by rail / train today.
Wir bedauern, Ihnen mitteilen zu müssen, dass ...	We regret having to tell / inform you that ...
Wir bedauern wirklich ...	We are really / indeed sorry ...
Bitte nehmen Sie unsere Entschuldigung entgegen.	Please accept our apologies.
Unsere Lieferanten waren nicht imstande, mit den Aufträgen Schritt zu halten.	Our suppliers found it impossible / were unable to keep up / pace with orders.
Die Nachfrage war so groß, dass ...	Demand was so great that ...
Unsere Vorräte sind erschöpft.	Our stock has been exhausted / used up.
Ein Feuer hat unsere Fabrik beschädigt.	A fire has damaged our plant.
Wir hoffen, dass Sie unsere Lage verstehen.	We trust / hope you will appreciate / understand our position.
Wir hoffen, dass diese Verzögerung Ihnen keine wesentlichen Unannehmlichkeiten verursachen wird.	We hope / trust that this delay will not cause you inconsiderable inconvenience.

Transport

Bitte befördern Sie die Waren sofort/ nicht später als .../per Lastwagen/ durch Luftfracht.	Please deliver the goods at once/not later than .../by road/by air.
Bitte nennen Sie uns den Namen des nächsten Schiffes nach ... und den letzten Termin, an dem Ladungen angenommen werden.	Please inform us as to the name of the next ship sailing to ... and the deadline for accepting cargo.
Bitte sorgen Sie dafür, dass die Waren nicht im Freien gelagert werden.	Please ensure that the goods are not stored in the open.
Bitte teilen Sie uns mit, wann und wie oft die Route gefahren wird.	Please let us have the times and frequency of your sailings.
Das Schiff muss am ... ladebereit sein.	The ship must be ready for loading on ...
Die Kartons haben die Abmessung ... und wiegen ...	The cartons measure ... and weigh ...
Die Waren werden in Kartons verpackt.	The goods will be packed in cartons.
Ihr Unternehmen unterhält einen Containerdienst.	Your company operates a container service.
Nennen Sie uns bitte Ihre niedrigsten Tarife.	Please quote us your lowest rates.
Unsere Packanweisungen müssen genau beachtet werden.	Our packing instructions must be strictly observed.
Wir brauchen ein Schiff mit einer Ladekapazität von ... Tonnen.	We require/need a ship with a cargo capacity of ... tons.
Wir haben erfahren, dass Sie einen weltweiten Frachtdienst anbieten.	We understand that you offer a global freight service.
Wir möchten ein Schiff chartern.	We want to charter a ship. **or** We wish to charter a vessel.
Wir werden uns um die Zollabfertigung kümmern	We will deal with the customs formalities ourselves. **or** We will attend to the customs formalities ourselves.

Zahlung und Mahnungen

Unsere Zahlungsbedingungen sind: ...	Our terms of payment are as follows: ...
Vorauszahlung	Cash in advance
Per Nachnahme	Cash on delivery / COD
Zahlung bei Erhalt der Rechnung	Payment on receipt of invoice
Zahlung bei Erhalt der Waren	Payment on receipt of goods
Zahlung durch Bankwechsel	Payment by banker's draft
... Tage netto	... days net
Durch Wechsel mit ... Tagen Ziel	By bill of exchange, at ... days
Ich sehe dem Empfang Ihrer Zahlung über den Betrag entgegen.	I look forward to receiving your payment of the amount.
Die Waren sind in gutem Zustand angekommen.	The goods arrived in good condition.
Ich danke Ihnen für Ihre Lieferung und füge einen Scheck über den Betrag Ihrer Rechnung bei.	I thank you for your delivery and I enclose a cheque covering the amount of your invoice.
Wir haben den Betrag auf Ihr Konto in ... überwiesen.	We have transfered the amount / sum to your account in ...
Wir haben Zahlung in Höhe von ... durch die ... Bank in ... vorgenommen.	We have arranged payment through the ... Bank in ... for the amount of ...
Wir stellen mit Bedauern fest, dass ...	We note with regret that ... **or** It is with regret that we note that ...
Es ist schwer zu verstehen, warum ...	We are at a loss to understand ...
Wir können es nicht verstehen, warum Sie unsere Schreiben unbeantwortet ließen.	We fail to understand why you have not replied to our letter. **or** We do not understand the reason for your failure to answer our letter.
Trotz wiederholter dringender Bitten um Begleichung unserer Rechnung	Despite / inspite of repeated urgent requests for payment of our invoice

haben wir noch immer nichts von Ihnen gehört.	we have still received no reply from you. **or** Even though we have repeatedly sent you urgent requests for payment, we have yet to hear from you.
Sie werden sicher verstehen, dass wir nicht länger auf Bezahlung warten können.	You will surely appreciate the fact that we can wait no longer for payment. **or** You must clearly understand that we cannot be expected to wait any longer for payment.
Wir müssen auf Zahlung bestehen.	We must insist on payment.
Wir wären sehr dankbar für einen baldigen Ausgleich unserer Rechnung.	Could you please settle our invoices as soon as possible. **or** We would appreciate an early settlement of our invoice very much.
Wir werden unsere Rechtsanwälte anweisen, gerichtliche Schritte gegen Sie einzuleiten.	We will instruct our solicitors to start proceedings / take legal action against you.
Falls wir Ihren Scheck nicht innerhalb der nächsten ... erhalten, müssen wir die Angelegenheit unserem Rechtsanwalt übergeben.	Unless we receive your cheque within the following ... we see ourselves compelled to put the matter in the hands of our solicitor. **or** Should we not be in receipt of your cheque within the next ... days we will be forced to turn the matter over to our solicitor.
Bitte prüfen Sie den Kontoauszug und teilen Sie es uns mit, wenn Sie irgendwelche Unstimmigkeiten finden.	Please check the statement and inform us if there any discrepancies.

Antworten auf Mahnungen

Wir bedauern es sehr, nicht auf Ihre Briefe geantwortet zu haben.	We regret very much not having replied to your letters.
Wir bitten um Entschuldigung wegen der Verzögerung in der Beantwortung Ihrer Briefe vom ...	We wish to apologize for the delay in answering your letters dated ...
Es scheint, dass wir Ihre Zahlungsbedingungen nicht völlig verstanden haben.	It would appear that we have not fully understood your terms of payment.
Es tut uns äußerst leid, dass Sie auf die Zahlung warten mußten.	We are extremely sorry that you were forced to wait for payment. **or** We are very sorry indeed that you had to wait for payment.
Heute haben wir unsere Bank angewiesen, die Summe von ... auf Ihr Konto zu überweisen	We have today instructed our bank to transfer ... to your account.
Wir fügen einen Scheck über ... zum vollen Ausgleich Ihrer Rechnung bei.	Please find enclosed a cheque for ... in full settlement of your bill.
Infolge unvorhersehbarer Umstände war es uns unmöglich, Ihre letzte Rechnung laut dem Auftrag zu begleichen.	As a consequence of circumstances entirely beyond our control we were unable to settle your invoice in accordance with the order.
Wir bedauern sehr, Sie um Aufschub bitten zu müssen.	We regret having to request a respite.
Angesichts unserer Schwierigkeiten müssen wir Sie um eine Kreditverlängerung bitten.	In view of our problems, we are forced to ask for an extension of credit.
Unsere gegenwärtigen Schwierigkeiten sind nur vorübergehend.	Our current/present difficulties are only of a temporary nature.
Unsere Kunden kommen in letzter Zeit ihren Verpflichtungen schleppend nach.	Recently our customers have been slow in meeting their obligations.
Wir haben erhebliche Schwierigkeiten beim Einzug unserer Rechnungen.	We are experiencing great difficulty in collecting payment.

Das Geschäft geht schlecht.	Business has been slack.
Wir sind in Schwierigkeiten gekommen, weil unser Hauptkunde Konkurs gemacht hat.	We are in difficulties as our main customer has gone bankrupt.
Wir beabsichtigen, die Rechnung bis zum Ende des Monats zu begleichen.	We intended to pay the bill by the end of the month.
Wir werden die ausstehende Summe bis Ende dieses Monats begleichen.	We will clear the outstanding amount by the end of this month.
Wir werden alle Anstrengungen unternehmen, um die Rechnung bis Ende ... zu bezahlen.	We are making every effort to pay the bill by the end of ... **or** We are doing our utmost to settle the account by the end of ...
Wir bitten Sie, so freundlich zu sein, und uns noch einige Wochen bis zur Zahlung des Betrags zu gewähren.	Please be good enough to grant us a few further weeks in which to pay the amount.

Beschwerden

Wir müssen Ihnen leider mitteilen, dass ...	We are unfortunately forced to inform you that ... **or** Unfortunately, we have to tell you that ... **or** We regret to inform you that ... **or** Regretably, we must advise you that ...
Leider müssen wir wegen ... reklamieren.	Unfortunately we must complain about ...
Wir müssen darauf hinweisen, dass ...	We feel forced to point out that ... **or** We must draw your attention to the fact that ...
Wir müssen darauf bestehen, dass ...	We must insist that ...
Wir erwarten Ihre Antwort.	We look forward to your reply.

Kiste Nr. ... enthält Artikel, die wir nicht bestellt haben.	Crate no. ... contains items which we have not ordered.
Beim Öffnen der Kiste stellten wir fest, dass ...	On / Upon opening the crate we found that ...
Wir können diese Waren nicht akzeptieren, da ...	We cannot accept these goods as / since ...
Offensichtlich wurde ein Fehler gemacht.	It is clear / obvious that an error / mistake has been made.
Wir müssen uns über die nachlässige Verpackung beschweren.	We must complain about the unsatisfactory / careless manner of packing.
Die Sendung kam in mangelhaftem Zustand an.	The consignment arrived in a defective condition.
Die Waren waren bei der Anlieferung schwer beschädigt.	The goods were badly damaged when delivered.
Wir hoffen, dass ein solcher Fehler nicht wieder vorkommt.	We hope / trust that such an error will not occur / happen again.
Beim Wiegen des Sackes stellten wir fest, dass ... Kilo am Gewicht fehlen.	On / Upon weighing the bag we found that it was ... kilos underweight.
Wir müssen Sie davon unterrichten, dass wir uns über Ihre sonst ausgezeichnete Waren beschweren müssen.	We must notify / inform / advise you that we feel forced to complain about your otherwise / normally / usually excellent goods.
Die jetzige Sendung ist keineswegs zufriedenstellend.	The most recent consignment is totally / highly / completely unsatisfactory / unacceptable.
Leider sind die Geräte für den beabsichtigten Zweck völlig ungeeignet.	Unfortunately, the machines are totally unsuitable for the intended purpose.
Die Qualität des gelieferten Artikels entspricht bei weitem nicht der des Musters.	The quality of the item delivered fails to correspond to that of the sample whatsoever.
Wenn diese Sendung nicht bis ... hier eintrifft, sehen wir uns genötigt, den Auftrag zu stornieren, da wir nicht länger auf die Geräte warten können.	Should the consignment fail to arrive here by ..., we see ourselves forced to cancel the order since we cannot wait for the machines any longer.

Bankangelegenheiten

Bitte eröffnen Sie ein Konto.	Please open an account.
Bitte schließen Sie das Konto Nr. ...	Please close account no. ...
Wir wären dankbar, wenn sie uns einen Kredit von ... gewähren würden.	We would be grateful if you would arrange a credit of ...
Bitte gewähren Sie uns ein Darlehen von ... für die Zeit von ...	Please allow us a loan of ... for a period of ...
Bitte veranlassen Sie die Überweisung von ... am ersten dieses Monats.	Please arrange the transfer the amount of ... on the first of this month.
Bitte überweisen Sie ... von unserem laufenden Konto bei Ihrer Geschäftsstelle auf das Konto der Firma ... bei Ihrer Zweigstelle in ...	Please be kind enough to transfer ... from our account at your branch to the account of ... at your ... branch.
Bitte sperren Sie die Zahlung des obigen Schecks.	Please stop payment of the above cheque.
Bitte stellen Sie mit Wirkung vom ... die monatlichen Zahlung an ...	Please cease / discontinue / cancel the monthly payments to ... with effect from ...
Der Scheck ist anscheinend in der Post verlorengegangen.	The cheque seems / appears to have been lost in he post.

Bewerbungen

Ich beziehe mich auf Ihre Anzeige in ... vom ...	With reference to you advertisement in ... dated ...
Ich bewerbe mich um den Posten eines ...	I am applying for the post of a ...
Ich möchte mich um die Stelle bewerben.	I should / would like to apply for the post.
Ich habe von ... gehört, dass in Ihrer Abteilung die Stelle eines Verkäufers frei ist.	I understand from ... that there is an opening for a sales man in your department. **or** ... has led me to understand that you are seeking to fill a vacancy for a sales man in your department

Augenblicklich bin ich als Buchhalter tätig.	At the moment I am employed as an accountant. **or** At present I work as a book keeper.
Augenblicklich bin ich arbeitslos.	At the moment I am out of work. **or** At present I am seeking employment. **or** I am between jobs for the time being. **or** I am, at the moment, looking for a position.
Während der letzten vier Jahre ...	During the last four years ...
Eine Firma Ihrer Größe bietet mir bessere Möglichkeiten/Aussichten.	A large company like yours offers better/improved opportunities/prospects.
Ich möchte meine jetzige Stelle aufgeben, weil ich hier nur beschränkte Möglichkeiten habe, verantwortungsvolle Tätigkeiten zu übernehmen.	I wish to leave my present post as I see only limited opportunities of assuming more responsibilities. **or** I would like to give up my current position since it presents very few possiblities for assuming greater responsibility.
Ich besuchte ... die Schule/Universität ... Jahre lang.	I attended ... school/university for ... years.
1985 schloß ich meine Ausbildung an der Universität ab.	I graduated in 1985.
Vom ... bis ... habe ich bei der Firma ... in ... meine Ausbildung erhalten.	From the year ... to the year ... I served an apprenticeship with ... in ...
Ich habe gute Russischkenntnisse	I have a good/fair knowledge of Russian
Ich spreche fließend Arabisch und Französisch.	I speak fluent Arabic and French.

Ich wäre äußerst dankbar, wenn Sie mir ein Vorstellungsgespräch gewähren würden.	I should / would be extremely grateful if I could have an interview. **or** I would appreciate it very much if you granted me an interview.
Ich wäre für die Möglichkeit eines Vorstellungsgesprächs dankbar.	I would appreciate the opportunity of having an interview.
Ich werde sehr gerne zu einem Vorstellungsgespräch kommen.	I should be most pleased to attend an interview.
Ich werde am ... verfügbar sein.	I shall be available on ...
Ich sehe dem Erhalt einer positiven Antwort gerne entgegen.	I look forward to receiving a positive / favourable reply.

Termine und Einladungen

Am Dienstag, dem ... werde ich wieder in ... sein.	I shall / will be again be in ... on Tuesday ...
Bitte schlagen Sie einen anderen Tag / eine andere Zeit vor, falls diese Zeit / dieser Tag Ihnen nicht passt.	Please suggest an alternative day / time if this time / date does not suit you.
Bitte rufen Sie mich an.	Please give me a ring.
Eine Nachricht wird mich im Büro erreichen.	A message will reach me in the office.
Ich freue mich darauf, Sie wieder zu sehen.	It will be a pleasure to see you again.
Ich freue mich sehr, Sie zu treffen.	I will be delighted to meet you.
Ich freue mich, Sie zu treffen.	I look forward to meeting you.
Ich würde die Gelegenheit begrüßen, das Problem mit Ihnen persönlich zu besprechen.	I would / should welcome the chance / opportunity of discussing the problem with you personally.
Ich würde die Gelegenheit, Sie zu treffen, schätzen, um Einzelheiten zu besprechen.	I would appreciate the chance / opportunity of meeting / seeing / getting together with you in order to discuss details.

Ich würde mich freuen, wenn Sie eine Zeit und ein Datum vorschlagen würden, um ...	I would be pleased / happy / glad if you would suggest a time and date to ...
Ich würde Sie gerne aufsuchen ...	I would like to call on you ...
Vielleicht könnten Sie sich mit mir so bald wie möglich in Verbindung setzen.	Perhaps it would be possible for you to get in touch with me as soon as you can. **or** Maybe you could contact me as soon as possible.
Wäre es überhaupt möglich, einen anderen Termin zu vereinbaren?	Would it be at all possible to arrange another meeting?
Wenn Sie mich anrufen, wäre es vielleicht möglich, einen Termin irgendwann im nächsten Monat zu vereinbaren.	If you rang me up / gave me a ring it would be perhaps possible to sort out / fix / arrange a meeting sometime next month.
Würde Ihnen ... um ... passen?	Would ... on ... suit you? **or** Would ... on ... be convenient?
Ein Termin am Nachmittag würde mir besser passen.	An afternoon appointment / meeting would suit me best.
Ich werde die ganze Woche im ... Hotel sein, und eine Nachricht wird mich hier sicher erreichen.	I shall be spending the whole week at the ... Hotel where a message will certainly reach me.
Leider muß ich das vereinbarte Zusammentreffen für den ... verschieben.	Unfortunately I will have to postpone / put off the appointment made for ...
Leider müssen wir das Zusammentreffen am nächsten ... absagen.	We are sorry but we must cancel the meeting planned for next ...
Herr ... bedauert sehr, dass er nicht in seinem Büro war, als Ihr Vertreter gestern vorbeikam.	Mr ... regrets it very much but he was not in the office when your representative called.
Er wurde unerwartet zu der Fabrik in ... gerufen.	He was unexpectedly called over to the plant in ...

Vielen Dank für Ihre freundliche Einladung.	Thank you very much for your kind invitation.
Es hat mich äußerst gefreut, Ihrem Brief vom ... zu entnehmen, dass Sie und Ihr Mann in März in ... sein werden.	I was most pleased to learn from your letter dated ... that you and your husband will be in ... in March.

Niederlassungen planen

Wenn Sie Ihre Firma hierher verlegen, bieten sich mehrere Vorteile.	Moving your company here will result in several advantages.
Es gibt gute Straßen und Bahnverbindungen.	There are good road and rail connections.
Die Regierung wird Anreize bieten.	The government will offer incentives.
Grundstücke können gepachtet werden.	Sites are available for rent.
Sie können die Grundstücke besichtigen.	You can inspect the sites.
Es gibt Fabriken, die zu sofortiger Nutzung zur Verfügung stehen.	There are factories available for immediate use.
Falls Sie Ihre Fabrik erweitern möchten, wird es kein Problem geben, da angrenzendes Bauland verfügbar ist.	If you wish to expand your factory there will be no problem as there is building land adjoining.
Sonderfinanzierungen werden gewährt.	Special loans are available.

VOCABULARY

A

ability	*Fähigkeit*
able; be ~ to do	*etwas können*
abroad	*im Ausland*
accept	*annehmen*
accept a draft	*einen Wechsel akzeptieren*
acceptance	*Annahme*
accommodation	*Unterkunft*
accompany	*begleiten*
accordance; in ~ with	*gemäß, entsprechend*
according to	*entsprechend*
accordingly	*dementsprechend*
account	*Rechnung, Konto*
accountant	*Buchhalter*
accounts department	*Buchhaltungsabteilung*
accustomed to	*gewöhnt daran*
acknowledgement	*Bestätigung, Auftragsbestätigung*
act as an agent	*als Agent arbeiten*
actually	*eigentlich, in der Tat*
addition; in ~	*außerdem*
admit	*zugeben*
advance; in ~	*im voraus*
advantage	*Vorteil*
advertise	*annoncieren, Werbung machen*
advertisement	*Annonce, Anzeige*
advise	*verständigen, unterrichten, beraten*
agency	*Agentur*
agency agreement	*Vertretervertrag*
agent	*Vertreter*
agreed	*vereinbart*
agreed; as ~	*wie vereinbart*
agreed condition	*vereinbarte Bedingung*
allow	*gewähren*
although	*obwohl*

amount	*Betrag*
annul	*annullieren*
anyway	*trotzdem*
apart from	*abgesehen von*
apologise	*sich entschuldigen*
applicant	*Bewerber*
application	*Bewerbung*
apply for	*bewerben um*
apply on spec	*sich auf gut Glück bewerben*
appoint	*ernennen*
appreciate	*zu schätzen wissen, gerne zur Kenntnis nehmen*
appreciative	*dankbar*
area	*Gebiet*
arrival	*Ankunft*
arrive	*ankommen*
as a result of	*als Folge*
as far as ... is concerned	*was ... betrifft*
as soon as	*so bald wie*
as well as	*sowie*
assistance	*Hilfe*
assume	*annehmen*
assure	*versichern*
assure; ~ somebody of something	*jemandem etwas versichern*
at all	*überhaupt*
at least	*mindestens*
at the latest	*spätestens*
attach	*beiheften*
attached	*beigeheftet, beiliegend*
attention (draw attention to something)	*Aufmerksamkeit (auf etwas lenken)*
attention; for the ~ of...	*zu Händen von ...*
attention; your order will receive ~	*Ihre Bestellung wird bearbeitet*
attention; it has come to our ~	*wir sind darauf aufmerksam geworden*
availability	*Vorrätigkeit*
available	*vorrätig, lieferbar*
avoid	*vermeiden*

B

badly bruised (fruit)	*(Obst) mit schlimmen Druckstellen*
balance	*Kontostand, Saldo ausgleichen*
balance sheet	*Bilanz*
banking	*Bankwesen*
basic	*einfach*
believe	*glauben*
bend	*Bogen*
bet	*wetten*
beyond our control	*nicht in unserer Hand liegend*
bill	*Rechnung*
bill of exchange	*übertragbare Zahlungsanweisung, Wechsel*
bill of lading	*Seefrachtbrief/Konnossement*
biscuit	*Keks*
board of directors	*Vorstand*
booth	*Stand*
boring	*langweilig*
box	*Karton*
bracket	*Anschluß*
branch	*Filiale*
breach of contract	*Vertragsbruch*
brochure	*Prospekt*
builder	*Bauunternehmer*
bulk order	*Großauftrag*
business practice	*Geschäftspraxis*
business relationship	*Geschäftsbeziehung*
buyer	*Käufer, Einkäufer*
by the same post	*mit gleicher Post*

C

caller	*Anrufer*
cancel	*stornieren*
cancellation	*Stornierung*
candidature	*Kandidatur*
cargo	*Fracht*
carry out	*ausführen*
case	*Kiste; Fall*
cash discount	*Skonto*

catalogue	*Katalog*
cause	*verursachen/Ursache*
cautious	*vorsichtig*
certain	*bestimmt*
certainly not	*sicher nicht*
certificate	*Zeugnis*
Chamber of Industry and Commerce	*Industrie- und Handelskammer*
chap	*Kerl*
charge; in ~	*verantwortlich*
charity	*Wohltätigkeitsverein*
charming	*charmant*
chat me up	*mich anquatschen*
cheap	*billig*
chief	*Haupt-*
CIF (Cost, Insurance, Freight)	*Kosten, Versicherung, Fracht*
circumstance	*Umstand*
clear	*begleichen*
clear a bill	*eine Rechnung begleichen*
clearly	*offensichtlich*
clerk	*Büroangestellte*
close to	*in der Nähe von*
clothing	*Kleidung*
coal	*Kohle*
collect payment	*einziehen, Inkasso durchführen*
come up to	*entsprechen*
common	*gemeinsam*
comparison	*Vergleich*
compel	*zwingen*
competition	*Konkurrenz*
competitive	*konkurrenzfähig*
complain	*beklagen, Beschwerde einlegen*
complaint	*Beschwerde*
complete	*ausführen*
complete a form	*ein Formular ausfüllen*
concern	*Sorge, Besorgnis*
concerning	*bezüglich, hinsichtlich*
condition	*Bedingung*
condition of payment	*Zahlungsbedingung*
confidence	*Vertrauen*

confidential	*vertraulich*
confirm	*bestätigen*
consequence	*Folge*
consequence; as a ~	*als Folge*
consider	*denken, betrachten, glauben*
considerable	*groß, erheblich, beträchtlich*
considerable; with ~ regret	*mit großem Bedauern*
consideration; take into ~	*in Betracht ziehen*
consignment	*Lieferung, Sendung*
contact	*sich in Verbindung setzen*
contain	*enthalten*
Continent	*Kontinentaleuropa*
contract	*Vertrag*
contribute	*beitragen*
convenient time	*passende Zeit*
convinced; to be ~	*sicher sein, überzeugt sein*
copper pipe	*Kupferrohr*
corner shop	*Laden an der Ecke*
correspond	*entsprechen*
council	*Verwaltung*
counter-offer	*Gegenangebot*
couple of	*ein paar*
courtesy	*Höflichkeit*
cover for	*einspringen für*
covering letter	*Begleitbrief*
crate	*Kiste*
credit enquiry agency	*Kreditauskunftei*
credit facility	*Kreditrahmen*
creditworthiness	*Kreditwürdigkeit*
curious	*neugierig*
current	*aktuell*
current account	*laufendes Konto*
curriculum vitae (CV)	*Lebenslauf*
custom	*Kundschaft*
customer	*Kunde*
customs	*Zoll*
cut the costs	*die Kosten reduzieren*

D

dad	*Papa*
damaged	*beschädigt*
darling	*Schatz, Liebling*
dated	*datiert*
dates ... to ...	*vom ... bis zum ...*
day off	*Tag frei*
deadline	*letzter Termin*
deal with	*fertig werden mit*
debts	*Schulden*
decide	*entscheiden; sich ~*
defective	*fehlerhaft, defekt*
delay	*Verspätung, Verzögerung*
delighted	*entzückt*
delivery	*Lieferung*
delivery date	*Liefertermin*
delivery time	*Lieferfrist*
demand	*Nachfrage*
department	*Abteilung*
departure	*Abreise*
depending on	*abhängig von*
depending on	*hier: je nachdem*
deposit	*deponieren/Einlage, Guthaben*
despatch	*senden, versenden*
despatch advice	*Versandanzeige*
despite the fact that	*trotz der Tatsache, dass*
develop	*entwickeln*
develop a market	*einen Markt erschließen*
direct debit	*Einzugsermächtigung*
disappointed	*enttäuscht*
discount	*Rabatt*
display (on display)	*Ausstellung (ausgestellt sein)*
disposal; placed at the ~	*zur Verfügung gestellt*
disposal; at my disposal ~	*zu meiner Verfügung*
disregard	*ignorieren, nicht beachten*
distribute	*verteilen*
distribution	*Verteilung*
distributor	*Verteiler, Großhändler*
diving equipment	*Tauchgeräte*
do business	*Geschäfte machen*

domestic market	*Binnenmarkt*
don't worry	*keine Sorge*
draft	*Tratte, gezogener Wechsel*
dreadful	*schrecklich*
dried dates	*getrocknete Datteln*
drive me round the bend	*mich verrückt machen*
due	*fällig*
due to	*aufgrund, infolge, wegen*
due; the goods are ~ to arrive on the ...	*die Waren sollen eintreffen am ...*
duration	*Dauer*
duty	*Pflicht*

E

early order discount	*Frühdispositionsrabatt*
education	*Ausbildung*
effect	*ausführen*
elsewhere	*anderswo*
embassy	*Botschaft*
employed	*beschäftigt sein*
employee	*Arbeitnehmer*
enclose	*beilegen*
enclosed	*beiliegend*
enquire	*fragen, erkundigen*
enquirer	*Fragesteller*
enquiry	*Anfrage*
enterprising	*unternehmungslustig*
entirely	*völlig*
equipment	*Geräte, Ausrüstung*
error	*Fehler*
especially	*besonders*
essential	*sehr wichtig*
establish	*gründen, bilden*
estimate	*schätzen*
evaluate	*einschätzen, beurteilen*
excess; in ~ of	*mehr als übersteigend*
excuse	*Ausrede*
execute	*ausführen*
execute orders	*Bestellungen ausführen*

execution	*Ausführung*
exhibition	*Ausstellung*
expanding	*expandierend*
expectations	*Erwartungen*
expensive	*teuer*
experience	*Erfahrung*
experienced	*erfahren*
explain	*erklären*
explanation	*Erklärung*
extension	*Verlängerung*
extremely	*äußerst*

F

facility	*Einrichtung, Möglichkeit*
factory	*Fabrik*
fail to do	*etwas nicht tun, etwas unterlassen*
failure	*Misserfolg, Scheitern*
faith; in good ~	*in gutem Glauben*
familiar	*vertraut*
favour; in your favour ~	*zu Ihren Gunsten*
filing cabinet	*Aktenschrank*
fill in	*ausfüllen*
final demand	*letzte Mahnung*
finalize	*endgültig festlegen*
finally	*endlich*
firm	*bestimmt, fest, streng*
fix up	*arrangieren*
following	*folgende*
food	*Lebensmittel*
force	*zwingen*
force; ~ somebody to do something	*jemanden zwingen, etwas zu tun*
foreign language	*Fremdsprache*
foreign trade	*Außenhandel*
form	*Formular*
forward	*befördern, senden*
forwarding agent	*Spediteur*
freight rate	*Frachtsatz*

frozen	*blockiert*
fulfil	*erfüllen*
furnish with something	*mit etwas versorgen*
further	*weiter*
future	*Zukunft*

G

GCE A Level	*Abitur*
GCE O Level	*mittlere Reife*
general public	*Publikum, Öffentlichkeit*
generate (be generated)	*entstehen*
get about	*viel herumkommen*
get a name	*bekannt werden*
get in touch with	*sich in Verbindung setzen*
glad	*froh*
go slow	*Bummelstreik*
going on (what is going on)	*was los ist*
good grief!	*mein Gott!*
good mood	*gute Laune*
good time; in ~	*rechtzeitig*
good will	*Wohlwollen*
goods	*Waren*
grant	*gewähren*
grant an agency	*eine Vertretung übertragen*
grateful	*dankbar*

H

hairy	*haarig*
handle	*bearbeiten*
hangover	*Kater*
have a go at something	*versuchen, etwas zu tun*
have trouble	*Probleme haben*
head	*Leiter*
head of sales	*Leiter der Verkaufsabteilung*
heating engineer	*Heizungsinstallateur*
heating equipment	*Heizgerät*
hesitate	*zögern*

hire	*einstellen*
hold on!	*Moment mal!*
hold the view that	*der Ansicht sein*
hold up	*verspäten/Verspätung*
hopefully	*hoffentlich*
hopeless	*hoffnungslos*
however	*jedoch*

I'd better	*ich sollte, es wäre besser*
ice skating	*Eislauf*
illustrated literature	*Bildmaterial*
immediate	*sofortig*
importance	*Wichtigkeit*
impression	*Eindruck*
in general	*im allgemeinen*
in the black	*in den schwarzen Zahlen*
in the press	*in der Presse*
in the red	*in den roten Zahlen*
in this case	*in diesem Fall*
in writing	*schriftlich*
in your favour	*zu Ihren Gunsten*
inability	*Unfähigkeit*
incentive	*Anreiz*
include	*einschließen*
including	*einschließlich*
inconvenience	*Unbequemlichkeit, Unannehmlichkeit*
incredible	*unglaublich*
indicate	*deuten auf*
industrial action	*Arbeitskampfmaßnahmen*
influence	*beeinflussen*
inspect	*besichtigen*
inspection	*Kontrolle*
instead of	*anstelle von, statt*
instruct	*anweisen*
instruction/instruct	*Anweisung/anweisen*
insurance	*Versicherung*
insurance certificate	*Versicherungszertifikat*

insurance policy	*Versicherungspolice*
intend	*beabsichtigen*
interest (rate of interest)	*Zinsen (Zinssatz)*
interview	*Vorstellungsgespräch*
investigate	*überprüfen*
invitation / invite	*Einladung, einladen*
invoice	*Warenrechnung*
involved	*beteiligt*
issue a letter of credit	*ein Akkreditiv ausstellen*
item	*Artikel*

J

joint owner	*Mitbesitzer*
junior	*Bürogehilfe*

K

keep up with	*Schritt halten mit*
kindly	*freundlicherweise*

L

law	*Gesetz*
law; go to ~	*vor Gericht gehen*
lazy	*faul*
lead to	*dazu führen*
leading	*führend, wichtig*
legal action	*Klage*
legal proceedings	*Verfahren, Gerichtsverhandlung*
legally binding	*verbindlich*
lending department	*Kreditabteilung*
let down	*enttäuschen*
let somebody have something	*jemandem etwas schicken*
let us have	*schicken Sie uns*
letter of credit	*Akkreditiv, Kreditbrief*
level	*Ebene*
libel	*Verleumdung*
limited	*beschränkt*

line	*Branche*
lined with styrofoam	*mit Schaumstoff ausgekleidet*
list	*auflisten*
loan	*Darlehen*
local government	*Kommunalverwaltung*
local market	*örtlicher Markt*
locate something	*etwas finden*
location	*Lage, Örtlichkeit*
look for	*suchen nach*
look forward to	*sich freuen auf*
look into	*prüfen*
loss	*Verlust*
lost	*verloren*
luckily	*zum Glück*

M

make it (can you make it?)	*schaffen (schaffen Sie es?)*
make up	*Zusammensetzung*
mark	*beschriften*
market a product	*etwas auf den Markt bringen*
matter	*Sache, Angelegenheit*
meet; ~ a date	*einen Termin einhalten*
meet up	*treffen*
member	*Mitglied*
mention	*erwähnen*
message	*Nachricht*
ministry	*Ministerium*
misunderstanding	*Missverständnis*
monk	*Mönch*

N

need	*Bedürfnis*
neighbouring	*angrenzend, benachbart*
note	*zur Kenntnis nehmen*
number	*nummerieren*

O	obtain	*bekommen, erhalten*
	occasion	*Gelegenheit, Anlass*
	occur	*vorkommen, passieren*
	offer	*Angebot/anbieten*
	old-fashioned	*altmodisch*
	on my arrival	*bei meiner Ankunft*
	on receipt	*nach Eingang*
	on time	*pünktlich*
	opinion; be of the ~	*der Meinung sein*
	opportunity	*Möglichkeit*
	order	*Auftrag*
	order book	*Auftragsbuch*
	order form	*Bestellformular*
	outstanding	*ausstehend*
	overdraft	*Überziehung*
	overdraw	*überziehen*
	overdue	*überfällig*
	overlook	*übersehen*
	overripe	*überreif*
	overseas	*Übersee*
	overseas market	*Überseemarkt*
	oversight	*Versehen*
	overtime	*Überstunden*
	owing to	*infolge*
	owner	*Besitzer*

P	participate	*teilnehmen*
	participation	*Teilnahme*
	pass	*vergehen*
	past	*vergangen*
	pay up	*zurückzahlen*
	payable	*zahlbar*
	payment	*Zahlung*
	perform	*leisten, durchführen*
	performance	*Leistung*
	perishable	*leicht verderblich*
	pick up	*abholen*

pipe	*Rohr*
place an order	*einen Auftrag erteilen*
plant	*Anlage, Fabrik*
pleased to	*sich freuen*
point out	*hinweisen auf, betonen*
polite	*höflich*
pompous	*schwülstig*
port of call	*Anlaufhafen*
post	*Stelle*
postage	*Porto*
practice	*Gewohnheit, Verfahrensweise*
precise	*genau*
prepared	*bereit*
previous	*vorherig, vorhergehend, früher*
price list	*Preisliste*
pride	*Stolz*
prior to	*vor, bevor*
priority	*Vorrang*
probably	*wahrscheinlich*
promise	*Versprechen*
promote	*fördern*
proposal	*Vorschlag*
prospect	*Aussicht*
prove	*beweisen*
provide	*liefern*
provide with	*mit etwas versorgen*
pull somebody's leg	*jemanden auf den Arm nehmen*
punctuation	*Zeichensetzung*
purchasing department	*Einkaufsabteilung*
put forward	*vorschlagen*
put in touch / contact	*sich in Verbindung setzen*

Q

quantity discount	*Mengenrabatt*
query	*Frage*
quid (slang for pound)	*Eier (Slang für Geld)*
quota	*Kontingent*
quotation	*Kostenvoranschlag, Preisangabe*

R

raise	*Gehaltserhöhung*
range	*Sortiment, Auswahl*
rate	*Satz, Kurs*
ready market; find a ~	*einen guten Markt finden*
reason	*Vernunft; Grund*
receipt; in ~	*im Besitz*
receive	*erhalten*
recent	*neulich*
reception	*Empfang*
refer to	*sich beziehen auf*
reference	*Referenz, Zeugnis*
refund	*zurückzahlen*
regarding	*in bezug auf*
regret	*bedauern*
regrettably	*bedauerlicherweise*
regular	*regelmäßig*
regular order	*regelmäßiger Auftrag*
relation	*Beziehung*
relationship	*Beziehung*
relative	*Verwandte*
reliable	*zuverlässig*
remark	*Bemerkung*
remind somebody of	*erinnern; jemanden ~ an*
remittance	*Zahlung*
rent	*mieten*
replacement	*Ersatz*
reply	*antworten/Antwort*
report	*berichten/Bericht*
representative	*Vertreter*
reputable	*seriös, solide*
request	*bitten, ersuchen/Bitte*
require	*benötigen, erfordern*
requirement	*Bedarf, Bedürfnis*
respected	*angesehen*
response	*Antwort*
result in	*führen zu*
retailer	*Einzelhändler*
right	*Recht*
right	*richtig*
rise	*Erhöhung (Geld)*
risky	*riskant*

S

sail	*abfahren, auslaufen*
sales condition	*Verkaufsbedingung*
sales department	*Verkaufsabteilung*
sample	*Muster*
satisfy	*zufriedenstellen*
saturated	*gesättigt*
savings account	*Sparkonto*
security	*Sicherheit*
seller	*Verkäufer*
service	*Dienstleistung*
set up	*gründen, einrichten*
settle	*erledigen, klären*
settle a bill	*begleichen*
settlement	*Bezahlung*
ship	*versenden, verschiffen/Schiff*
shipment	*Sendung, Verschiffung*
shipowner	*Reederei*
shipping agent	*Reedereivertreter*
shipping documents	*Versanddokumente*
shipping instructions	*Versandanweisungen*
shop steward	*Arbeitnehmervertreter*
shorthand	*Kurzschrift*
shortly	*bald*
sight draft	*Sichtwechsel*
site	*Gelände, Stelle, Grundstück*
situations vacant	*Stellenangebote*
size	*Größe*
slander	*Beleidigung*
slightly	*etwas, ein kleines bisschen*
slip of paper	*Blatt Papier*
smart	*schick*
solicit	*verlangen*
solicitor	*Anwalt*
solvency	*Zahlungsfähigkeit*
sort out	*erledigen*
space	*Platz, Raum*
spare no effort	*keine Mühe scheuen*
special delivery	*Sonderlieferung*
spelling	*Rechtschreibung*
spelling mistake	*Rechtschreibfehler*

spoilt	*verdorben*
spot	*Stelle*
square	*Viereck*
stand	*Stand*
stand in	*einspringen, vertreten*
standing	*Ruf*
standing; of many years' ~	*mit einem langjährigen guten Ruf*
standing order	*Dauerauftrag*
stay	*Aufenthalt*
stay competitive	*konkurrenzfähig bleiben*
stock; from ~	*ab Lager*
stock; in ~	*auf Lager*
store	*Lager*
stress	*betonen*
strictest	*strengstens*
strictly	*streng*
subject to change without notice	*Preisänderung vorbehalten*
submit	*einreichen, unterbreiten*
subsidiary	*Tochtergesellschaft*
substantial	*wesentlich*
success	*Erfolg*
successful	*erfolgreich*
sufficient	*ausreichend*
suggest	*vorschlagen*
suggestion	*Vorschlag*
suitable	*geeignet*
supplier	*Lieferant*
supply	*beliefern*
suppose	*annehmen, vermuten*
surprise	*überraschen*
surprised	*überrascht*
suspend an account	*ein Konto sperren*

T

T-joint	*T-Stück*
take action	*etwas unternehmen, Schritte unternehmen*
take part	*teilnehmen*
tariff	*Zoll*

temporary	*vorübergehend*
term	*Bedingung*
terminate	*lösen, beenden*
terms of payment	*Zahlungsbedingungen*
think up	*erfinden, ausdenken*
thorough	*gründlich*
threaten	*drohen*
timber	*Holz, Bauholz*
tin of baked beans	*Dose mit gebackenen Bohnen*
to call attention to	*auf etwas aufmerksam machen*
tools	*Werkzeuge*
to our satisfaction	*zu unserer Zufriedenheit*
trade	*Handel, Geschäft*
trade discount	*Händlerrabatt*
trade fair	*Handelsmesse*
trade reference	*Handelsreferenz*
trainee	*Auszubildender*
transaction	*Geschäft, Transaktion, Abwicklung*
transfer	*überweisen/Überweisung*
transport cost	*Transportkosten*
treat	*behandeln*
triplet	*Drilling*
tropical disease	*tropische Krankheit*
truck	*Lastwagen*
trusted	*vertrauenswürdig*

U

unable	*unfähig*
underweight	*untergewichtig*
union	*Gewerkschaft*
unit	*Einheit*
unless	*es sei denn, wenn nicht*
unreliable	*unzuverlässig*
unsatisfactory	*nicht zufriedenstellend*
unsolicited	*unverlangt, nicht bestellt*
untidy	*unordentlich*
upon; ~ opening	*bei (beim Öffnen)*
urgently	*dringend*
useful	*nützlich*

V

vacancy	*freie Stelle*
valid	*gültig*
valid until	*gültig bis*
valuable	*wertvoll*
variety	*Vielfalt, Auswahl*
various	*verschieden*
virtually	*nahezu, fast*
vital	*lebenswichtig*
vitals	*lebenswichtige Organe*
voluntary work	*freiwillige Arbeit*
vouch for	*sich verbürgen für*

W

wage	*Lohn*
waste	*verschwenden*
water pumps	*Wasserpumpe*
weed out	*aussieben*
weigh	*wiegen*
well established	*gut eingeführt*
what on earth!	*was in aller Welt!*
what's more	*außerdem*
whatever	*wie auch immer*
wholesale	*Großhandel*
wholesaler	*Großhändler*
wide range	*große Auswahl*
willing to	*bereit zu*
with a view to	*mit der Absicht, etwas zu tun*
with regard to	*hinsichtlich, in Bezug auf*
withdraw	*abheben*
withdraw an offer	*ein Angebot zurückziehen*
without engagement	*ohne Verpflichtung*
word gets round that ...	*man munkelt, dass ...*
work to rule	*Dienst nach Vorschrift*
wrong (what's wrong?)	*falsch (was ist los?)*

KEY TO THE EXERCISES

CHAPTER 1

Brain Work One: Let's practise style

1. Thank you very much for
2. If we purchase in excess of
3. In addition to this
4. were of inferior quality
5. We will be forced to find
6. an alternative supplier
7. to provide us with the goods

Brain Work Two: Quiz time

1. Yours sincerely
2. Dear Sir/Madam, Dear Sirs, Dear Sir or Madam
3. Yours faithfully
4. Dear Sir or Madam
5. (to start) Dear Mr Stecker, (to end) Yours sincerely

Brain Work Three: Test your word power!

Dear Mr Hudson

Thank you very much for your letter *dated* 20th November in which you say that you can *supply* us with any spare parts for our taxis. We are happy to *note* that you can send these parts next *week.*

We must point out that if the parts are of *inferior* quality we will be forced to *cancel* the order and find an alternative supplier.

We are sure you *understand* the situation.

Yours sincerely

A Pacino

CHAPTER 2

Brain Work One: What's the English for ...?

1. Please inform us / Please let us know
2. If your prices are competitive / If your prices are favourable
3. If your goods come up to our expectations / If your goods meet with our approval
4. We saw your advertisement in ...
5. Please make us an offer for ...

Brain Work Two: Complete the letter

a – **4.** grateful
b – **5.** concerning
c – **7.** quotation
d – **9.** enclosed
e – **2.** in addition
f – **6.** terms
g – **8.** substantial
h – **3.** competitive
i – **1.** approval

Brain Work Three: Be polite!

Please note that there are several possible answers to these exercises.

1. Could you please let us have / send us brochures about your tools?
2. Would it be possible for you to let us have your terms this week?
3. Could you please tell us what types of discounts you offer?
4. We were wondering if it might be possible for you to send us details about your wines and spirits?
5. Could / Would you please quote your prices CIF Melbourne?
6. Could / Would you please let us have / send us delivery dates and discount details?

Brain Work Four: Now you find the errors!

Dear Mr Hudson

We *visited* your stand at the Birmingham Exhibition Centre last week. We *were* most interested in the discussion that we had with you and the brochures that we *took* away with us.

We *supply* hotel chains on the Spanish mainland and Balearic Islands with office furniture and we *are* currently seeking alternative suppliers.
We are also interested to note that you *have* your own European transport department making delivery more accurate and quicker and that you could *deliver* to us directly.
Please let us *have* a quotation for 35 office chairs type 'Manager' in blue cloth covering, 15 office desks Type T84 and 20 filing cabinets Type F18.
Additionally *please inform* us as to delivery times and terms of payment as well as types of discount *offered* for large and frequent orders.
If your prices *are* competitive and the delivery times, terms of payment and quality of products meet with our approval we will be happy to place substantial orders regularly.
We *are looking/look* forward to a prompt response.
Yours sincerely
Phillip Sanchez

Here are notes on the corrections because verb tenses are very important.

'We *visited* your stand last week' and 'we *took* away with us'. Simple past tense about something that ended in the past and you say when it happened.
'We *were* most interested' last week but she / he / it was.
'We *supply* hotel chains here' means that generally we do this but not at the moment, not exactly this second. 'We supplied hotel chains' means we did but perhaps no longer, we have stopped.
'We *are* currently seeking' means we are doing this now.
'You *have* your own European transport department' means at this time you have or own a transport department.
'You *could deliver* to us directly' means in the future you can deliver or there is a possibility to deliver to us.
'Please let us *have* a quotation'. Here the verb 'let' is always followed by a verb in infinitive form like 'Let me go!' or 'Let's go for a drink!'
'Additionally *please inform* us' is the same as 'let' above, 'Please tell me your name.'
'Types of discount *offered*' is an example of the passive. Another example: 'the desks we make' or passive 'the desks made (by us)'.
'If your prices *are* competitive' is plural, many prices *are* but one price *is*.
'We are *looking/look* forward to'. Now or generally we are positive about getting an answer soon. It cannot be past here.

CHAPTER 3

Brain Work One: Sort out the letter

The order of the sentences in the letter should be:

b Dear Mr Wilson
d We were pleased to receive your enquiry dated ...
e As requested we are sending you a catalogue and price list
g We are also pleased to grant you a discount of 10% for an early order
f Please note that this offer and discount is valid for two weeks
c We look forward to the pleasure of doing business with you
a Yours sincerely

Brain Work Two: What's the English for ...?

1. – e, 2. – f, 3. – d, 4. – a, 5. – b, 6. – c

Brain Work Three: Replace the short forms

1. *We are* sending you information as requested
2. Your order *will* receive immediate attention
3. *We would* like a special discount
4. He *did not* send the letter on Tuesday
5. *It is* very expensive
6. The firm *has not* granted a discount

Brain Work Four: A little puzzle with vocabulary

1. supplier – Lieferant
2. brochure – Prospekt
3. catalogue – Katalog
4. offer – Angebot
5. request – Bitte
6. sample – Muster

CHAPTER 4

Brain Work One: Sort out a letter

The order of the sentences in the letter should be:

1. **f** Dear Mrs. Jackson
2. **c** We were pleased to receive your quotation of 12th May
3. **d** Kindly supply us with five kilos of first quality English Tea
4. **e** Please arrange an early delivery and notify us as soon as the goods are shipped
5. **b** We shall place further orders with you if this order is satisfactorily executed
6. **a** Yours sincerely

Brain Work Two: What's the English for ...?

1. – c, 2. – f, 3. – b, 4. – g, 5. – a, 6. – d

Brain Work Three: Put in the right words

1. payable, **2.** quotation, **3.** point, **4.** place, **5.** irrevocable, **6.** satisfaction

Brain Work Four: See if you see the mistake

1. We are very *pleased* to receive your quotation.
2. We will *place* further orders with you.
3. We will order more bags from you if they *are* good quality.
4. I look forward to *receiving* the samples.
5. Thank you for the *information* about the motor.
6. I *have* tested the product and am happy to send an order.

CHAPTER 5

Brain Work One: What's the English for ...?

1. – f, 2. – g, 3. – a, 4. – e, 5. – b, 6. – d, 7. – c

Brain Work Two: Put in the missing letters

1. sufficient, **2.** advise, **3.** payment, **4.** consignment, **5.** successful, **6.** delivery

Brain Work Three: Complete the letter

a – 3, b – 5, c – 4, d – 8, e – 6, f – 2, g – 7, h – 1

Brain Work Four: You construct a good letter

We wish to thank you for your order no. 55729 for office 257 filing cabinets type F18. We are happy to accept the order at the price stated by you along with your other terms.
We have sufficient cabinets in stock and can deliver by the date given. Shipment will be organised as soon as our bank advises us that payment arranged. The consignment will be shipped on MS Nostromo sailing from Lisbon 21st May and due to arrive on 29th May in Port Elizabeth.
We are certain that this is the start of a successful business relationship. We look forward to hearing from you in the near future.

CHAPTER 6

Brain Work One: A little letter writing

1. sorry, **2.** executing, **3.** delay, **4.** damaged, **5.** position, **6.** assure, **7.** despatch

Brain Work Two: Quiz time

1. – c, **2.** – a, **3.** – a, **4.** – b, **5.** – b, **6.** – a

Brain Work Three: How much do you understand?

1. The delay is 15 days.
2. 'four forklift trucks' or the 'delivery of four forklift trucks'
3. 'We sincerely apologise for the inconvenience caused.'
4. A machine at the / their supplier's plant.
5. 'set back' and 'hold up'
6. Production was set back slightly / a little by the late arrival of some components which was caused by the breakdown of a machine at a / the supplier's plant. Additionally / also / as well orders have been rather heavy over recent months.
7. 'additionally' and 'plant'
8. 'betonen'

Brain Work Four: You construct a letter

Dear Mr Hudson
We sincerely regret the delay in delivery of 5 days and the inconvenience caused you. This was due to production problems at our supplier's plant. The goods have already been despatched and will reach you within the next two days.
Yours sincerely
J Woodward

CHAPTER 7

Brain Work One: Complete the sentences

1. attach, **2.** instructed, **3.** execute, **4.** valid, **5.** confirmed

Brain Work Two: True or False?

1. F, 2. T, 3. T, 4. F

Brain Work Three: Letter writing

1. enclosing, **2.** instructed, **3.** open, **4.** irrevocable, **5.** valid, **6.** confirmed, **7.** agent

Brain Work Four: Put the sentences in order

1. We wish to inform you that we have arranged payment through the Royal Dutch Bank for the amount of $120.000.
2. Please note that we will transfer the £380 to your account next Friday.
3. Our terms are cash on delivery.
4. I am pleased to inform you that all items arrived in good condition.
5. I enclose a cheque covering the amount of your bill.
6. As soon as payment is made we will despatch your order.

Brain Work Five: How much do you understand

1. Letter One 'consignment' and Letter Two 'shipment'
2. Letter One 'by bank transfer as arranged to your account' and Letter Two 'In payment of your invoice we are sending a cheque'.

3. 'to confirm receipt of payment' or 'in confirmation of payment'
4. Letter One 'we would appreciate it' and Letter Two 'we would be grateful'
5. 'we have examined the items'
6. Mr Hudson informed the writer of Letter One that the shipment/ consignment had been sent.
7. 'in order' or 'in good order'

CHAPTER 8

Brain Work One: Over to you – letter writing

The order of the sentences in the letter should be:

2. Dear Mr Free
6. We should like to remind you that payment for order No 439B is a month overdue
4. Please find a copy of your invoice attached
5. An early settlement of this account would be appreciated
1. We look forward to hearing from you in the next few days
7. If you have already sent a remittance please disregard this letter
5. Yours sincerely

Brain Work Two: What's the English for ...?

1. Payment was *due* a month ago
2. Could you please *clear/pay/settle* your account as soon as possible?
3. Please *disregard/ignore* this letter if you have already cleared the account
4. Thank you for the *settlement/payment* of the bill
5. The *invoice* has not yet been paid
6. Please see the *attached* account

Key to Brain Work Three: Read and answer the questions

1. the current brochure and price list
2. 'you have overlooked this invoice'
3. That prices have not increased from last year's and that products remain the most competitive on the market in terms of both quality and price and also that they have extended their/the product range.

4. They look/he looks forward to receiving an order (from the customer) shortly.
5. 'settle'
6. The customer has (no doubt) overlooked this invoice.
7. Yes because 'you normally settle your account with us promptly'.
8. 'to enclose' or 'to send enclosed'

Brain Work Four: How much do you understand

1. 'we wish to point out'
2. 'the bill is now five weeks overdue'
3. one on 14th and one on 21st August
4. 'we are at a loss to understand'
5. No but 28th August is the last day. Payment can be made before because it says 'settlement by 28th August' not 'on 28th August'.

CHAPTER 9

Brain Work One: Complete the letter

1. reminders, **2.** insist, **3.** solicitor, **4.** Regrettably, **5.** outstanding, **6.** remittance

Brain Work Two: What's the English for ...?

1. remittance – Zahlung, **2.** concerning – bezüglich,
3. delay – Verzögerung, **4.** outstanding – ausstehend,
5. unless – es sei denn

Brain Work Three: Quiz time

1. – b, 2. – b, 3. – b, 4. – b

Brain Work Four: A little work on "by" and "until"

1. by, **2.** until, **3.** until, **4.** by, **5.** by

Brain Work Five: Please correct the errors

Dear Mr Crook

This is the third *occasion* that we have *written* to you to concerning the outstanding balance for £4,789 for order No 6719.

We had *expected* that you would have paid the bill *by* now but you have sent us no remittance or offered us no explanation *for* the delay.

Regrettably, *unless* you *make* the payment within the next seven *days* we will be *forced* to put the matter in the hands of our legal department.

Yours sincerely

Edward Nicely

Brain Work Six: Using new vocabulary

1. **b** We are at a loss to understand why the payment has not been made.
2. **c** If the cheque fails to arrive within seven days we will contact our solicitor
3. **d** Please explain why you have sent no remittance.
4. **e** We have written to you on two occasions concerning the outstanding balance.
5. **a** Unless we receive the remittance we will put the matter in the hands of our legal team.
6. **f** We are unhappy concerning the outstanding account.

CHAPTER 10

Brain Work One: What's the English for …?

1. – c, **2.** – d, **3.** – b, **4.** – e, **5.** – f, **6.** – a

Brain Work Two: Complete the sentences

1. receive, **2.** beyond, **3.** enclose, **4.** inconvenience, **5.** assure

Brain Work Three: A little translating

We regret very much the delay in payment of your *invoice/bill* No B527 for £102.50. The reason for the *delay/hold up* is that *we are having difficulties* because our *customers have recently been slow to meet their obligations.*

We *assure* you that our *present/current difficulties* are only *temporary* and that we will clear the *outstanding* amount *by the end of this month.*
Yours faithfully

Brain Work Four: Improve your powers to see mistakes

We regret very much the delay in *delivery*.
We *are* in difficulties as our main customer has gone bankrupt.
The reason for the delay *was* beyond our control.
We are *making* every effort to pay the bill by Tuesday of next week.
Please find a cheque *for* £200 enclosed.
We are happy to grant you two more *weeks* in which to deliver.

CHAPTER 11

Brain Work One: A little quiz

1. – b, 2. – c, 3. – a, 4. – c, 5. – b

Brain Work Two: Sort out the letter

The order of the sentences in the letter should be:

2. We are forced to complain about the delay in our order No D546.
4. You assured us that the goods would be here within a week.
1. That was three weeks ago.
5. The delay puts us in a difficult position as we need the goods urgently.
3. We will be compelled to cancel the consignment if the goods do not arrive by next week.
6. We will be pleased to receive your explanation.

Brain Work Three: Test your vocabulary

1. overdue – überfällig
2. execution – Ausführung
3. ship – versenden
4. urgently – dringend
5. confidence – Vertrauen
6. essential – sehr wichtig

CHAPTER 12

Brain Work One: What's the English for ...?

1. convenient – passend,
2. grateful – dankbar,
3. opportunity – Möglichkeit,
4. although – obwohl,
5. arrival – Ankunft,
6. prior to – vor/bevor

Brain Work Two: Letter writing

Dear Mr Barker
I would welcome the opportunity to meet you some time next week.
Would 10 o'clock on Tuesday be convenient? If this day and time are not convenient *please suggest an alternative time and day.* Please contact me in the company. If I am out *a message will reach me in the office.*
I am looking forward to meeting you again.
Your sincerely

Brain Work Three: Prepositions of time

1. in, **2.** on, **3.** at, **4.** in, **5.** in, **6.** on, **7.** at

Brain Work Four: A little puzzle with vocabulary

1. I look forward to seeing you.
2. We would like to call on you.
3. Please suggest an alternative date.
4. Please give me a ring as soon as you arrive.
5. I would welcome the opportunity of meeting you.
6. It would be possible to arrange another meeting next month.

CHAPTER 13

Brain Work One: What's the English for ...?

1. – b, **2.** – d, **3.** – e, **4.** – f, **5.** – a, **6.** – c

Brain Work Two: Complete the sentences

1. unfortunately, **2.** convenient, **3.** kind, **4.** owing, **5.** afraid, **6.** expect

Brain Work Three: Let's look at a few words

1. invitation – Einladung
2. opportunity – Möglichkeit
3. response – Antwort
4. overseas – Übersee
5. accommodation – Unterkunft
6. performance – Leistung

Brain Work Four: A little translation work

I should very much appreciate it if I could have the *chance* of meeting you on my *forthcoming visit* to Palma. I will be in Palma from Monday 9th April until Thursday 12th where I will be staying at the hotel 'Azul Verano'. *I shall contact your office by telephone on my arrival.* I would be grateful if you could *let me know* the day and time which would best *suit* you but I would prefer the afternoon of Wednesday 10th. If the day and time suggested *are inconvenient* please let me know and suggest another date for a meeting.
I look forward *to the pleasure* of seeing you and your production team then.

CHAPTER 14

Brain Work One: What's the English for...?

1. complain
2. point out
3. I must insist that
4. go to law
5. on opening
6. oversight
7. with regard to

Brain Work Two: Complete the letter

1. point out, **2.** upon, **3.** mistake, **4.** instead, **5.** inconvenience, **6.** as soon as

Brain Work Three: Quiz time

1. – a, 2. – b, 3. – a, 4. – b, 5. – a, 6. – b

Brain Work Four: You construct a good letter

Dear Sirs
We regret to inform you that on receiving order number P8829 we were most disappointed.
Firstly crate no. 5 contained items that we did not order. Crate no. 3 contained items, which were damaged and cannot be sold. Lastly crate no. 2 had parts missing.
It is very clear that a mistake has been made.
Clearly we must insist that these errors are rectified as soon as possible.
We look forward to your prompt reply.
Yours faithfully

CHAPTER 15

Brain Work One: Complete the letter

1. reference, **2.** slip, **3.** information, **4.** reliable, **5.** consider, **6.** grant, **7.** discretion, **8.** assistance

Brain Work Two: Words from the chapter

1. previous – vorherig / vorhergehend
2. standing – Ruf
3. recent – neulich
4. solvency – Zahlungsfähigkeit
5. confidential – vertraulich
6. creditworthy – kreditwürdig

Brain Work Three: Quiz time

1. T, 2. F, 3. F, 4. F, 5. F, 6. T

Brain Work Four: Finding and correcting mistakes

Dear Sirs
The company *mentioned* on the slip attached *has* given your name to us. Could you please let us *have* information regarding the credit standing of the firm? *Do* you consider it safe to *grant* a credit of about £25,000?
We wish to *thank* you very much for your co-operation and any information provided *will* be treated in the strictest confidence.
Yours faithfully

Brain Work Five: A little more translation work

1. You were named as a reference.
2. The firm is reliable and sound.
3. Can you give us / let us have information about this firm?
4. One / you should treat the information with discretion.
5. I hope that I can help you / be of assistance to you in a similar case.

CHAPTER 16

Brain Work One: Test your memory

1. – c, **2.** – f, **3.** – d, **4.**– e, **5.** – a, **6.** – b

Brain Work Two: Complete the letter

1. attention, **2.** staged, **3.** exhibited, **4.** deadline, **5.** space, **6.** cancel, **7.** fees, **8.** forward

Brain Work Three: Quiz time

1. – a, **2.** – b, **3.** – c, **4.** – a, **5.** – a, **6.** – c

Brain Work Four: You construct a letter

1. We would like to exhibit our products at the fair.
2. Please tell us the deadline for the applications.
3. We must remove our stand by Friday.
4. Can we cancel our application?
5. We will refund the fees.

6. You can put up your stand on Monday / You can put your stand up on Monday / On Monday you can put up your stand / On Monday you can put your stand up.

Brain Work Five: How much do you understand?

1. from the Internet
2. prior / prior to
3. wheel chairs
4. conditions of participation
5. electrical motors for lifts and cranes
6. promote

CHAPTER 17

Brain Work One: Complete the letter

We are writing to ask *you to grant us a loan of £20,000 for 12 months / for a period of 12 months.*
We need / require the loan to buy new machines for our factory. We are sure that as *customers* of many years you will agree we are a creditworthy company.
As security we can offer you share certificates worth £25,000.
If you wish to discuss the *matter, I would be ready* to visit you *at the bank.*
Yours faithfully

Brain Work Two: Memory test

1. overdraft – Überziehung
2. account – Konto
3. current account – laufendes Konto
4. transfer – überweisen
5. loan – Darlehen
6. cheque – Scheck

Brain Work Three: Word power building

1. If you are *in the red* it means you have less than zero in the bank.
2. To *transfer* money means to move it from one account to another.
3. When I say *deposit* money I mean put it in an account for example.
4. I could not use an account, which was *frozen.*
5. A *standing order* is a system where the bank pays any regular / monthly bills for you.
6. If a bank gives me a *loan* I must pay the money back within a certain time.

CHAPTER 18

Brain Work One: A little translation work

Dear Mrs Duffy
I wish to apply for the post as accountant which was advertised in the Daily Echo dated 23rd November 20.. . As you can see from my curriculum vitae *I am, at present/currently, employed as an accountant at Humble and Thwackit.* Although I am happy here, *I wish to apply for a post with more responsibility.* I would also like to widen my experiences a*nd improve my prospects for promotion.*
I will be pleased to send you *further* information and *I am available for interview by arrangement.*
Yours sincerely
Victoria Hope

Brain Work Two: Correct the spelling mistakes

deplartmint – department
dited – dated
ablikation – application
clean – keen
respkcted – respected
rfreees – referees
wouch – vouch
oppertuniti – opportunity
interwiew – interview
Blease – Please
kontakt – contact
rigardink – regarding

Brain Work Three: Test your vocabulary

1 – f, 2 – c, 3 – b, 4 – a, 5 – d, 6 – e

Brain Work Four: You construct a letter

1. I wish to apply for the post of teacher.
2. I will be happy to attend an interview.
3. At present I am employed in the accounts department at Peabody & Sons.

4. I would like to work in a position with more responsibility.
5. The main reason for my application is that I do not wish to work in the evenings.
6. Please consider my application for the post as receptionist.

CHAPTER 19

Brain Work One: Pick out the correct word

1. branches, 2. sole agent, 3. valuable, 4. experienced, 5. knowledge

Brain Work Two: Quiz time

1. – b, 2. – b, 3. – b, 4. – a, 5. – b, 6. – a

Brain Work Three: How much can you understand?

1. It is a major distributor of office furniture / It distributes office furniture
2. outlets
3. No, the firm has more than three. It has shops in all large cities including Barcelona, Madrid and Granada.
4. It found information on the Internet from a web site.
5. Yes, they have worked happily and successfully for other British firms acting as their agents.
6. 'We will do our utmost to further the sale of your products locally'.

CHAPTER 20

Brain Work One: Translate some parts

Dear Sirs
We have *found/learnt that your firm offers a container service.*
Our company needs to send 54 diesel motors to Istanbul and we would like a quotation for your current *freight rates. The goods are packed in crates and measure 1 meter 50 cm x (by) 1 meter 20 cm x (by) 2 meters and weigh 1258 kg.*
Please let us have the times and frequency of your sailings *and please let us have the name of the ship and the last date/deadline for accepting cargo.*
Yours faithfully

Brain Work Two: Test your prepositions

1. by, **2.** in, **3.** in, **4.** on, **5.** by, **6.** with

Brain Work Three: Sort out mixed up sentences

1. The goods will be packed in wooden crates.
2. Please observe the packing instructions.
3. We wish to charter a ship to Lisbon.
4. Please quote us the lowest rates.
5. We will hire a container for our move to Qatar.
6. Please let us have the times of your flights.

Brain Work Four: Test your error finding talent

Dear Ms Katzer
We are most pleased to *inform* you that the ceramics have *been* despatched as arranged. The pots have been packed in 21 *wooden* crates. The *crates* are marked GD in a green square and are numbered 1 to 21. The shipment will arrive in Hull on 11th September on the Argo, which *sailed* from Gibraltar this *morning*.
All shipping documents have *been* sent to Barclays Bank in Halifax.
We are convinced that our ceramic goods will *sell* very well and we *hope* you will *contact* us in the near future with further orders.
Yours sincerely
A. Martinez

CHAPTER 21

Brain Work One: Memory work

1. – f, **2.** – d, **3.** – a, **4.** – e, **5.** – b, **6.** – c

Brain Work Two: Quiz time

1. – a, **2.** – b, **3.** – b, **4.** – b, **5.** – b, **6.** – b

Brain Work Three: Build up your word power

Dear Mr Crook

We are *writing* to you as the head of the council in your town as we wish to *establish* a distribution *base* in your town. We are an American firm, which *produces* office furniture in Spain. *Due to* the fact that the market is *expanding* dramatically in Britain we wish to have offices, a parking area for trucks, *storage facility* and small factory there.

This will result in *jobs* for over sixty people at first but if the business expands there could be over one hundred *employees.*

We have a site in mind on the Hinckley Industrial Park. We are *keen on* this site because you are building a new road from it to the A68 road. We will also wish to *extend* the building so that we can *assemble* our office furniture there prior to *distribution.*

Please send us information on any financial *assistance* or any other incentives.

Yours faithfully

G. Trueman

Brain Work Four: Test your vocabulary!

1. Mr Crook offered us a large *incentive* to move to Nuneaton.
2. There are many *sites* for building available in this town.
3. We want to *extend* the building for storage.
4. Hudson International is a large firm with *branches* in Southern Europe.
5. Onions wants to set *up* a production facility in Sydney.
6. Telford makes special *loans* to companies who bring jobs to the town.

CHAPTER 22

Brain Work One: Correct the letter

Dear Mr Peabody

This is to thank you *most sincerely* and warmly for the excellent *hospitality* you extended to me.

It was indeed wonderful to have this possibility *of meeting* you and your managers.

I *hope* and look forward to being able to receive a *visit* from you here in England.

Yours sincerely

Fred Dolittle

Brain Work Two: Put in the words

1. extending, **2.** sincerely, **3.** promotion, **4.** take, **5.** pleasure,
6. reciprocating

Brain Work Three: Writing a letter

I am writing this letter to say that I was most pleased to have the opportunity of meeting you at your factory in Wolverhampton. I feel that this meeting will be very beneficial for future business contacts. I hope that you will give us the chance of inviting you to see us in Belgrade. Once again many thanks.

Brain Work Four: Build up your vocabulary!

1.	**d**	once again	nochmals
2.	**c**	take the opportunity	die Gelegenheit ergreifen
3.	**b**	extend hospitality	Gastfreundschaft erweisen
4.	**f**	promotion	Beförderung
5.	**e**	pave the way	den Weg ebnen
6.	**h**	things are looking up	es geht bergauf
7.	**a**	bring to fruition	aufblühen lassen
8.	**g**	look after	sich kümmern um

CHAPTER 23

Brain Work One: A quiz on using emails

1. **a**, **b** and **d** are correct, **c** and **e** are not correct.
2. **c** is correct.
3. 'Best regards, All the best, Yours respectfully' are fine for emails. 'Cheers' and 'bfn' are rather too informal. 'Sincerely yours' is too formal and 'Bottoms up' is said only with a drink in your hand!
4. The answer is **c**.

Brain Work Two: Can you change your style of writing?

These are suggested answers.

1. Thanks a lot for the info you sent us.
2. We must tell you that the goods were lost in transit.

3. Please feel free to call / Call us if you have any questions about our products.
4. We are very sad to tell you that ...
5. Please tell us by phone when you want to drop by.

Brain Work Three: A little grammar exercise

These are suggested answers.

1. Sand has damaged the goods.
2. Our manager, Mrs Oldfield, will visit you in May.
3. Our despatch department will pack the pumps in wooden crates.
4. When we opened the boxes we found that you had made a mistake.
5. I / we posted the letter last Friday.
6. I'm sorry but I can't be at the meeting.
7. We are talking about the problem at Friday's meeting.
8. If you order more than 500 we will grant a discount of 25 per cent.

rororo
Illustration: Cathrin Günther

Illustration: Cathrin Günther

René Bosewitz/Robert Kleinschroth
Get Through at Meetings
Business English für Konferenzen und Präsentationen.
Buch mit Tonkassette
3-499-60266-0

René Bosewitz/Robert Kleinschroth
How to Communicate Effectively
Verstehen und verstanden werden im Business
3-499-61146-5

René Bosewitz/Robert Kleinschroth
How to Phone Effectively
Business English am Telefon.
3-499-60139-7/61449-9
Buch mit Audio-CD
3-499-60146-X/64156-1
Buch mit Tonkassette
3-499-60147-8

René Bosewitz/Robert Kleinschroth
Idioms at Work
Bessere Geschäfte mit treffendem Englisch
3-499-61333-6

René Bosewitz/Robert Kleinschroth
Manage in English
Business rund um die Firma
3-499-60137-0

René Bosewitz/Robert Kleinschroth
Master Your Business Phrases
Sprachmodule für den Geschäftsalltag
3-499-60725-5

3-499-61146-X

6066/1